Volume 14　　　　　**Number 1**　　　　　**2018**

Journal of
Character Education

Jacques S. Benninga
Marvin W. Berkowitz
Editors

Jonathan M. Tirrell
Managing Editor

INFORMATION AGE
PUBLISHING

JOURNAL OF CHARACTER EDUCATION

EDITORS

Jacques S. Benninga, *California State University, Fresno*
Marvin W. Berkowitz, *University of Missouri—St. Louis*

EDITORIAL BOARD

Sheldon Berman, *Andover (MA) Public Schools*
Melinda Bier, *University of Missouri–St. Louis*
Shelley H. Billig, *RMC Research Corporation*
Ann Higgins D'Allesandro, *Fordham University*
Jonathan Cohen, *Teachers College, Columbia University*
Matthew Davidson, *Institute for Excellence and Ethics (NY)*
Maurice Elias, *Rutgers University*
Constance Flanagan, *University of Wisconsin-Madison*
Brian R. Flay, *Oregon State University*
Perry L. Glanzer, *Baylor University*
William Hansen, *Tanglewood Research*
Charles C. Haynes, *First Amendment Center*
John D. Hoge, *University of Georgia*
James Leming, *Character Evaluation Associates (FL)*
Thomas Lickona, *State University of New York–Cortland*
Marco Muñoz, *Jefferson (KY) County Public Schools*
Larry Nucci, *University of California at Berkeley*
Fritz Oser, *University of Fribourg*
Terry Pickeral, *Cascade Educational Consultants*
Clark Power, *University of Notre Dame*
Kevin Ryan, *Boston University*
Eric Schaps, *Developmental Studies Center*
Arthur Schwartz, *Widener University*
Scott Seider, *Boston University*
Bryan Sokol, *Saint Louis University*
Herbert J. Walberg, *University of Illinois at Chicago*
Lawrence J. Walker, *University of British Columbia*
Mary Williams, *La Salle University*
James Youniss, *Catholic University of America*

MANAGING EDITOR

Jonathan M. Tirrell, *Tufts University*

Journal of Character Education
Volume 14 • Number 1 • 2018

MISSION STATEMENT

The *Journal of Character Education* serves an audience of researchers, policymakers, teacher educators, and school practitioners concerned with the development of positive character in young people. Character.org defines character education as efforts to help young people develop good character, which includes knowing about, caring about, and acting on core ethical values such as fairness, honesty, compassion, responsibility, and respect for self and others. The editors and Character.org view character education as a comprehensive and interdisciplinary term that reflects Character.org's Eleven Principles of Effective Character Education. These principles call on schools to address character education in their overall school climate, academic curriculum, extracurricular activities, interpersonal relationships, and school governance. These efforts are school-wide and should touch every student and all school personnel. They can include both comprehensive school reform and more specific school-based efforts such as service learning, life skills education, conflict resolution and violence prevention, social and emotional learning, education for the prevention of drug/alcohol abuse, sex education, education for civic virtue and social responsibility, and the development of moral reasoning. Of clear relevance also are multicultural education, social justice education, the ethics of environmental or technology education, religious education, and the like. The Journal will publish articles that report the results of research relevant to character education, as well as conceptual articles that provide theoretical, historical, and philosophical perspectives on the field of character education as it is broadly defined above. The Journal is also interested in more practical articles about implementation and specific programs.

Directions to Contributors

All manuscripts submitted must conform to the style of the *Publication Manual of the American Psychological Association* (APA), 6th Edition. Manuscripts must be typewritten, double-spaced throughout with 1" to 1.5" margins all around. Manuscripts typically should run between 15–25 pages in length, excluding references. All manuscripts should include an abstract of 100–150 words and a separate title page that includes the name(s) and affiliation(s) of the authors, as well as contact information for the lead author: address, phone number, fax number, and e-mail address. Following preliminary editorial review, manuscripts are sent for blind review to reviewers who have expertise in the subject of the article. The title page will be removed before the manuscript is distributed to reviewers.

Manuscripts may be submitted by e-mail to jce@umsl.edu.

EDITORS' INTRODUCTION

As the editors of the *Journal of Character Education*, we are pleased to introduce the first issue of the journal's 14th volume. Nearly at the midpoint of its second decade, we wish to give credit and thanks to both our wonderful Managing Editor, Dr. Jonathan Tirrell, and a generous grant from the John Templeton Foundation that has provided complementary subscriptions to emerging scholars. We are always on the lookout for new subscribers and new manuscripts. You, our readers, are the best source of help with both.

In this issue, we have continued to focus both on peer-reviewed scholarly work and on editor-reviewed practitioner-focused manuscripts. In the latter category ("Voices"), we continue a recent tradition of publishing the comments by the most recent recipient of Character.org's "Sandy Award" (the Sanford N. McDonnell Lifetime Achievement Award in Character Education). In 2017 this prestigious award was given to longtime character.org leader Charles Haynes. We include here the introductory remarks of former Character.org Executive Director Linda McKay and the acceptance speech delivered at that ceremony by Dr. Haynes.

We often get requests from those who have created character education programs and/or curricula to publish evidence of their effectiveness; however, they rarely have a single study which meets the methodological criteria for scholarly publication. So we have tried a new strategy here for the first time. Joseph Hoedel and Robert Lee's article is a report that follows more the criterion of "a preponderance of evidence" (based on a series of studies over 15 years) than a single "gold standard" (e.g., randomized control design) single study. We will be interested in how readers react to this strategy, and we welcome your comments.

These papers are accompanied by three more excellent scholarly papers. Andrea Ettekal and colleagues present a study of the perspectives of high school athletic directors on character education. Sarah Hamsher reflects on the application of positive causal attribution training to character education. Toni Mandelbaum reports empirical data on the relation between attachment and grit in adolescence. In addition, Thomas Lickona's new book about parenting for character is reviewed by David Streight.

Thank you for your subscribership to the only journal devoted exclusively to character education and character education research.

Journal of Character Education, Volume 14(1), 2018, p. v
ISSN 1543-1223

The Character Exchange is Character.org's digital platform providing educators with the professional and personal development needed to improve school culture.

 Gain a deeper understanding through a certification in the *11 Principles of Effective Character Education.*

 Brainstorm and exchange ideas with an active community of practitioners and experts in the field of character education.

 Access a large and frequently updated resource center filled with Promising Practices and the latest research in character.

Visit **characterexchange.org** to start today!

THE 2017 CHARACTER.ORG "SANDY AWARD" REMARKS HONORING DR. CHARLES HAYNES

Linda McKay
Board Chair, Character.org

I am honored and pleased to be presenting the 2017 Sanford N. McDonnell Award for Lifetime Achievement in Character Education to a dear colleague and dear friend, Dr. Charles Haynes.

This award is named in honor of Charcter.org's Founding Chairman Sandy McDonnell, who upon retiring as chief executive officer and president of McDonnell Douglas in 1989 began a second 20-year career working tirelessly in advocacy and support for quality character education to be embraced by schools and communities. Through his words and actions, he was a role model of good character for all.

Since 1998 the Sandy Award has been given to people who have demonstrated a "long and steadfast commitment to the field of character education."

So I want to take this opportunity for others to learn about today's recipient Charles Haynes—a person who is well known and highly regarded in both the character education and civic education worlds for his long history of bringing together a wide range of groups with a wide range of beliefs to find common ground and work together for the common good.

Charles is founding director and former vice president of the Newseum Institute/Religious Freedom Center in Washington, DC where he also serves as senior scholar of the First Amendment Center, and syndicated columnist for "Inside the First Amendment."

It sounds like Charles has three jobs rather than just one.

Charles is best known for his efforts to successfully find common ground on First Amendment conflicts. Over the past 2 decades, he has been the principal organizer and drafter of consensus guidelines on religion and values in schools which have been endorsed by a broad range of religious, civil liberties, and education organizations.

He is the coauthor of six books including *First Freedoms: A Documentary of History of First Amendment Rights in America* and *Finding Common Ground: A First Amendment Guide to Religion and Public Schools.*

His column, "Inside the First Amendment" appears in newspapers nationwide. He is a national and international expert to whom educators, reporters, legislators and leaders from other countries turn to understand controversies regarding religion and public education.

Journal of Character Education, Volume 14(1), 2018, pp. 1–2
Copyright © 2018 Information Age Publishing, Inc.

ISSN 1543-1223

He has been profiled in *The Wall Street Journal* and on the *ABC Evening News*, and has made frequent appearances on television and radio including *The NewsHour with Jim Lehrer*, *The Today Show* on NBC, *CBS Evening News*, CNN, National Public Radio, and BBC.

His expertise has been widely quoted in newspapers and magazines, including the *New York Times*, *Washington Post*, *Los Angeles Times*, *Time,* and *Newsweek*

Charles does not just write about the importance of civic character. For decades he has joined with others to make it a reality. And Character.org has been the grateful recipient of Charles' longtime support.

As a founding member of Character.org, Charles was part of a group that decided a national organization should be formed to advocate for character education to be of critical importance for our students and the future of our communities. From day one Charles took an active part in the formation of what this organization should be.

As one of his nominators, Diane Berreth, said, "It is not an overstatement to say that Character.org would not have been formed without Charles' presence. His knowledge, thoughtfulness, and ability to bridge differences were critical to bringing together our first board and membership.

To this day Charles has continued to provide leadership as a member of the board.

It was Charles who led the effort to create the Eleven Principles of Effective Character Education, and develop the Schools of Character Recognition program, Character.org's flagship program. During his time as board chair he led the change to identify not just 10 schools but support as many schools as could meet the Schools of Character Eleven Principles.

In the closing, I share the words of Kristie Fink, a nominator for this award, who wrote, "It would be difficult to name a person who has worked longer or more tirelessly over the past 2 and half decades to build capacity in schools and organizations across the country to develop strong, lasting character education initiatives for the benefit of youth and our nations' institutions. In addition, Charles' work is always rooted in promoting rights and responsibilities for all, and he effectively models what he preaches."

KEEPERS OF THE NATION'S CONSCIENCE
Charles C. Haynes Acceptance Speech of the 2017 Sanford N. McDonnell Lifetime Achievement Award (the "Sandy Award")

KEEPERS OF THE NATION'S CONSCIENCE

To receive an award named for my dear friend and mentor, Sandy McDonnell, is the greatest honor of my life. Thank you Character.org for the privilege of supporting our extraordinary staff and serving with our dedicated board.

Let me take this opportunity to also thank family and friends, especially my beloved husband Christopher who gives me love and strength each day.

Since the founding of this organization some 24 years ago, schools and communities like those represented in this room today have done life-changing work to instill strong civic character in many thousands of young people in this country and around the globe. But we know that the work of building strong character is an ongoing effort, a commitment that must be renewed in each generation.

When thinking about how to lift up and celebrate our shared mission on this occasion, I returned yet again to a favorite quotation from Benjamin Franklin—written in a letter to a friend in the year the Constitution was drafted:

Only a virtuous people are capable of freedom. As nations become corrupt and vicious, they have more need of masters.

The first sentence is so often quoted, it has become a cliché of self-congratulation in a country that is often weak on self-reflection. But it is the *second* sentence that should give us pause. Franklin reminds us that our experiment in democracy and freedom is fragile. Absent civic virtue among the people, this experiment will surely fail.

No one is born with civic virtue; it must be continuously modeled and taught in our homes and schools. You know this or you would not be sitting here today. A great deal is at stake in the work that you do in classrooms across America. In no small measure, your work is what stands between us and the authoritarian rule and sectarian violence now enveloping much of the world.

I have fought all of my life for liberty of conscience—religious freedom—for people of all faiths or none. Today, more than three fourths of the world's people live in places with high restrictions of freedom of conscience, a condition that is the leading cause of oppression and violence across the globe.

As we gather here today, Rohingya Muslims are facing genocide in Burma, Christian communities are being obliterated in Iraq and Syria, Christians and Muslims are at war in northern Africa—and the tragic list goes on.

Journal of Character Education, Volume 14(1), 2018, pp. 3–5
Copyright © 2018 Information Age Publishing, Inc.
ISSN 1543-1223

And in this country, religious and political divisions are tearing us apart. White supremacy, Islamophobia, and anti-Semitism are surging, threatening to turn our public square into an angry, hostile, and even violent place.

If we seek to create a more peaceful world—if we aspire to build an America where people can live peacefully with their deepest differences—then we must fight to protect liberty of conscience, the freedom for each of us to follow our God, to follow what our deepest convictions require. This is what Roger Williams famously called "soul liberty."

But freedom is not sufficient. "Only a *virtuous* people are capable of freedom." That is why for the past 23 years my vocation has been liberty of conscience, but my avocation has been character education. Just as conscience requires freedom—so freedom requires conscience. Only people of conscience are capable of acting with compassion, making difficult moral decisions, and, in these ways and others, building a more just and free society.

The inseparable link between freedom and conscience was brought home to me most powerfully some years ago when I was standing in the Garden of the Righteous at Yad Vashem, the Holocaust memorial in Jerusalem. Our guide was relating stories of the Righteous—non-Jews who risked their lives to save Jews—as we looked at the trees planted in their honor.

During a pause in the narrative, one of our group, Richard Foltin of the American Jewish Committee, said almost inaudibly: "Not all of them are named." I turned and asked, "Richard, what do you mean?" He said: "I am standing here now because of a man whose name I do not know." When pressed to explain, he told this story:

"My parents are Holocaust survivors," he began. "When my father arrived at Auschwitz, they were separating those who would be killed immediately from those who would be put to work. A guard called out, 'Is anyone here a welder?' And my father shouted, 'I am'—although he actually knew nothing about welding. They sent my father and a few others

to the welding shop and told them to make a sample of their work for inspection. My father stood there looking at the equipment, despairing over what to do. Then, almost imperceptibly, the German foreman in charge of the shop slipped a finished piece of work in front of my father. My father picked it up and took it to the guards—and he passed inspection. Throughout the rest of his time in the camp, the foreman continued to secretly help my father—to cover for him when necessary. And my father survived. They didn't speak. We don't even know his name."

When Richard ended his story, I could not help but wonder: Why did that nameless German risk his life for a Jew he did not know? More broadly, why did any of the thousands—now called the Righteous—respond with compassion and courage when so many millions were either complicit or indifferent? Rescuers came from all walks of life, had varying degrees of education, some were religious and others were not. But they had one thing in common: when faced with a choice, they acted to save others—risking and in some cases losing their own lives. Only people of conscience have the courage to care in such extreme circumstances. They did not have time to think about it; they acted spontaneously from the heart.

Shaping the conscience of young people is what teachers and administrators committed to character education do every day. Together with parents, faith communities, and others, schools and classrooms of character are places where we model and teach the habits of the mind and heart that define people of good conscience. The test of conscience is not just in the life-threatening moments—the tests come every single day.

Who will stand up when a fellow student is harassed for wearing a headscarf? Who will step in when a transgender student is mocked and bullied? Who will speak up when students are called names, shamed, or shunned? By what you model and teach, you prepare young people to pass those tests—to have the courage to care. And by so doing, you prepare them to be citizens who will defend and protect freedom and democracy—not just for themselves, but also for others.

Yes, I want to see schools graduate people who can do the math, read the books, understand history and science. We need an educated citizenry. But I want even more to see schools graduate people with civic virtue and good character. What matters more than academic achievement is how people use what they know to serve the common good by working for a more just and free society. Germany in the 1930s, lest we forget, was arguably the most educated society in the world.

Some years ago, a reporter asked Justice Hugo Black—a former KKK member who became one of the 20th century's great defenders of human rights—to describe the role of the Supreme Court. "I believe," he replied, "that the Supreme Court is the keeper of the nation's conscience." That has a nice ring to it, especially when we recall such courageous and moral decisions as *Brown v. Board of Education.*

But as much as I appreciate the vital role of the High Court in upholding the Constitution, I would save that honorific for you—the teachers, counselors, administrators, staff members—who by what you do to instill civic virtue in our young people are the *true* keepers of our nation's conscience. Thank you for who you are—and for what you do each and every day.

Only a virtuous people are capable of freedom.

EMPIRICALLY INFORMED CHARACTER AND LEADERSHIP EDUCATION IN FOCUSED HIGH SCHOOL CLASSROOMS
15 Years of Consensus, Development, and Evaluation

Joseph M. Hoedel and Robert E. Lee
Character Development & Leadership

This 15-year program of research explored the extent to which prosocial attitudes and behavior of high school students were increased by focused lesson plans administered in dedicated high school classrooms over 1 or 2 academic semesters. The narrative describes the evolution of the Character Development and Leadership Program from a pilot study in 1 public high school to a curriculum employed by 2,000 high schools nationwide in traditional classrooms and online. First, a Delphi study provided empirically determined consensus about which character traits were most relevant to the needs of educators and students in the high school setting. This was followed by the development and evolution of a focused, highly structured classroom program to inculcate and strengthen these character traits for diverse students in socioculturally diverse high schools. Concurrent efficacy studies suggested that participating students consistently demonstrated a significant diminution of negative behavior outcomes and an increase in positive ones. These were differing kinds of studies in an exponentially growing number of real-life settings. Therefore not all data could be as complete as desired, comparison groups were not always available, and program fidelity was not always constant. Nevertheless, the evolving program and outcomes data make a composite case for the efficacy of the Character Development and Leadership Program and provide a practical illustration for other developers of empirically driven programs in character and leadership education.

Urged on by their legislatures and boards of education, many secondary schools in the United States have been searching for a comprehensive curriculum to inculcate ethical decisionmaking and leadership behavior throughout their student bodies (Davidson, Lickona, & Khmelkov, 2008).

Such a legislative mandate and two critical parameters shaped what would eventually become the Character Development and Leadership (CD&L) Program.

- The CD&L Program began in response to a challenge by a local high school

• **Correspondence concerning this article should be addressed to:** Joseph M. Hoedel, jhoedel@characterandleadership.com

Journal of Character Education, Volume 14(1), 2018, pp. 7–27
Copyright © 2018 Information Age Publishing, Inc.

principal. He perceived that his student body gradually had declined in the character traits and leadership behaviors that, in his opinion, drove a positive academic climate.

- He therefore wanted a direct hands-on approach to targeted high school students. He envisioned a course focused on character and leadership, one class period a day, for a semester. The first author was asked to develop that class and subsequently to teach it.

- This envisioned program would be a field study (cf. Fraenkel, Wallen, & Hyun, 2011). Because field studies occur in real-life settings they characteristically lack the situational refinements and comparisons of university human science laboratories. Therefore, they are said to assess "efficacy" as opposed to "effectiveness" (cf. Fedson, 1998; Godwin et al., 2003).

The program of scholarship described below is an example of the empirically based character education recommended by Berkowitz and Bier (2005, 2007). That is, it describes 15 years of developmental research "in the trenches". Because the projects assessed an evolving program in situ the level of full details was not always ideal. However, taken together these endeavors make a composite case for the efficacy of the CD&L Program and perhaps offer illustrations for other empirically oriented professionals to consider.

The narrative to follow describes three central developmental processes of the CD&L Program as it evolved from year 2000 through 2015, moving from a single high school elective course to manualized curricula (see Lee, 2014b) for the traditional classroom setting and also online. It currently is being used by over 2,000 high schools in the United States. These developmental processes were:

- Scientifically determined consensus about which character traits were most

relevant to the needs of educators and students in high school settings.

- The evolution of a focused classroom program to inculcate and grow these character traits, as well as leadership skills in diverse students in diverse high schools.

- Assessment of desired changes in students' thoughts, perceptions, and behaviors.

PROCESS ONE: A SCIENTIFICALLY DERIVED CONSENSUS ABOUT WHAT IS TO BE TAUGHT

The first step was to determine the specific character traits the intervention team (educators and content experts) considered to be most relevant to the educators' desired outcomes. The next step was to develop a corresponding list of specific, concrete behaviors presumed to reflect the presence of each trait in the educators' school and community contexts. These behavioral descriptions are called "operational definitions" of the traits, to wit, specific indicators to be observed and tallied. This foundation was crucial not only to the current application, but for credible extensions to future programs and the valid comparison within and between future schools. A Delphi methodology (cf. Turoff & Linstone, 2002) was adopted as an empirical way to arrive at consensus relevant to the educators' problem-centered goals. After all, comparable challenges in related fields of study had been neatly resolved using the Delphi method, for example, participatory action research in public health (Fletcher & Marchildon, 2011), innovative interventions in education planning (Helmer-Hirschberg, 1966), and financial forecasting (Green, Armstrong, & Graefe, 2007).

Method

Participants. The Delphi Method is a structured process for arriving at consensus through the use of a panel of experts. There-

TABLE 1

Members of the Delphi Panel of Experts (N = 19; 10 Males, 9 Females) Who Arrived at Consensus
About the Names and Behavioral Definitions of the 16 Most Relevant Character Traits
to be Taught to High School Students in a Semester Class

- An editor of a major academic family science journal
- The director of character education for a southeastern state, who also worked in that state's department of public instruction
- A leader in the field of character education with a proven track record of transforming school climate and improving the character of students
- An academic whose entire career was comprised of educational leadership positions at the undergraduate and graduate levels
- A family and child scientist at a research-intensive land grant university
- The long-term superintendent of a major school district in a southeastern state
- A principal of a high school with 30 years of experience
- The director of an at-risk mentoring program for middle-adolescent youth
- The director of a statewide fatherhood initiative with a background in family studies, adolescent development, and family therapy
- Two stay-at-home parents with a vested interest in their children's development
- Two youth ministers
- Six community stakeholders of various educational and vocational levels

fore, the experts had to be agreed upon and recruited. The program developers wanted the Delphi panel to be a credible mix of content experts (e.g., academicians specializing in character education in the schools), those with experience with the issues at hand (e.g., high school administrators and other professionals), and lay individuals with "skin in the game" (e.g., parents of high school students and concerned community members). Based on their professional contacts and collaborations, the high school principal and the senior author together recruited the members of their Delphi panel. The principal would subsequently be a member of the panel and the senior author would facilitate its processes. The 19 participants are listed in Table 1.

Procedure. The Delphi method is an empirical way of arriving at consensus through, first, generating information and, subsequently, distilling that information in systematic reiterative cycles. In the present study the panel members operated separately and returned their responses to the facilitator. The

first task each member was given was to answer the open-ended question: "What character traits do each of you consider 'most important' if adolescent males and females are to be successful in the ninth through 12th grades and in their communities?" A definition of each trait was also required. Their collective responses were compiled by the facilitator, who discovered that further refinement of this list of traits was necessary. Its large initial size (102 traits) was partially the result of connotative redundancy and overlap. Consequently, the panelists' individual lists were returned to each member with the instruction to provide behavioral examples of each trait, namely, "What specific observable behavior would indicate to you that this trait was in operation or lacking?"

Upon completion of that task, the facilitator eliminated clear redundancies (same label and same behavior) and then sent the remaining list of traits and alleged behavioral indicators back to the panel members. Each trait and its illustrative behavior was compared to every other trait in a paired-comparison presentation (David, 1988) using a 5-point Likert format ranging from "*very much alike*" to "*not at all alike.*" The subsequent statistical analysis indicated that some of these traits still could be assessing the same things. These traits were returned to the panel paired with a 5-point Likert scale ranging from "*very much the same*" to "*not at all the same.*" The result of this process was a short list of 32 traits and their behavioral indicators, all of which the panel members agreed were important to the success of high school students, both in the classroom and out of it.

At this point a critical parameter of the field study had to be addressed: A major contextual limitation was that one trait was to be the focus of each of 16 weeks in a semester, followed by a final 2 weeks of review and conclusions using the predetermined traits "Leadership" for week 17 and "Character" for week 18. Therefore, the panel members each subsequently rank ordered the list of 32 traits according to each member's opinion of a trait's importance to this population, in this school setting, with regard to outcome goals, and ease of recognition.

The entire Delphi process required 18 months. The panel members were unpaid volunteers. The convergence of their opinions resulted from systematic waves of questioning and statistical analyses. Common trends were recognized and outliers were conceptually integrated or set aside. Telephonic and email confrontation of disagreements resulted in constructive insights (Dick, 2000).

Results. The resulting character traits and their operational definitions are given in Table 2. They are not rank ordered according to their average rating. This listing is how they might fit into an 18-week curriculum (cf. Hoedel, 2010), fully understanding that the final two weeks would be "leadership" and "character" and used for consolidation.

The panel thought that the first six traits might be considered foundational, that is, the floor upon which citizenship could be constructed. The next six traits were focused on the skills necessary for positive character growth in the students' current social environments. The last four traits addressed what good citizenship would look like and be expressed in these students' futures.

Discussion

There was much basic agreement among the panelists by the time that the proposed traits reached the final stage. Certain traits did not make the final list simply because the number of usable weeks in a semester was limited and the proposed character education curriculum presupposed immersion in only one trait each week. Moreover, in debriefing sessions, some popular traits were eliminated because they were too difficult to define uniquely in discrete, observable behavior (e.g., "humility," civility," and "good judgment"). Some popular traits struck the panel as more elementary school oriented than high school appropriate (e.g., "compassion" replaced "kindness").

In Table 2, some traits appear to be synonymous. One such pair is "integrity" and "honesty." However, the panel decided that each was unique. Integrity was defined as an internalized set of values that guides decisionmaking processes. Honesty was considered concern for truthfulness in one's thoughts, responses, and behaviors, that is, the relative absence of lying, cheating, and stealing. Another apparently synonymous pair might be "appreciation" and "gratitude." In this pair the panelists wished to distinguish between recognizing, understanding, and accepting the value of role models in their sociocultural worlds as opposed to being aware of, valuing, and inclined to use these positive resources in their lives.

This consensus list of traits includes both "moral" and "performance" character traits (cf. Davidson, 2004). The importance of both categories has been argued compellingly and empirically demonstrated in high school students (Lickona & Davidson, 2005).

From the beginning of this program of study there has been a feedback loop between

TABLE 2

Summary of Delphi Panel Consensus: The 16 Most Important Character and Leadership Traits to be Taught to Ninth through 12th Graders and Their Average Rating (*SD* < .05) by 19 Panel Members

Character Trait	Average Rating	Definition in Mid-Adolescence	Behaviors Indicating the Presence or Absence of trait
"Foundational"			
Positive Attitude	10.0	Pro-social orientation, affirming belief systems, self-discipline	Optimism; internal causality; prosocial goals
Preparation	10.0	Priorities with realistic sub-goals	Articulating pathways to personal goals
Perseverance	10.0	Macro and micro steadfastness in school	Records of lateness, absences, completing assignments, preparation for tests; concern about grades
Respect	10.0	Good social judgment and deference to peers, educators, and self	Civility of behavior and words: Positive and negative behavioral incidents
Honesty	10.0	Respecting the truth as well as demonstrating it	Caring about and obtaining high reliability ratings by teachers and peers; The relative absence of lying, cheating, and stealing.
Integrity	10.0	Developing personal values	Owning thoughts, actions, and consequences; internal causality
"Skill Acquisition"			
Courage	9.8	Effective handling of peer group pressure; Defending beliefs and values	Recognizing skills for resisting negative peer pressure; constructive arguing in class
Appreciation	9.8	Recognizing role models and understanding their significance in one's life	Admiring specific role models from curriculum, school, community; Identifies with model
Composure	10.0	Effectively dealing with anger and aggression	Absence of disciplinary citations, and growth in the number of positive academic and social behaviors
Empathy	9.8	Positive communication skills	Demonstrating active listening (listen, clarify, confirm, and accept multiple realities)
Gratitude	9.8	Feeling grateful for external resources	Finding and using external resources; asking for help; expressing thanks
Compassion	9.8	Concerned awareness of peer victimization	Addressing incidents of bullying; helping, not hurting, potential targets
"Positive Futures"			
Tolerance	10.0	Demonstrating tolerance for diverse populations	Accepting multiple realities; Negative reactions to out-groups versus inclusion
Service	9.8	Putting welfare of others ahead of self	Considered to be an important value; Incidents of altruism and volunteering
Loyalty	9.8	Sustaining long-term relationships	Number of friends and length of friendship; Longest time held a job; Longest time in romantic relationship; School pride
Responsibility	9.8	Cultivating employability in the workplace	Showing initiative, being present and on time, completing assignments, grade point average

Note: The conceptual and operational definitions of each are included.

consumers and the author and his panelists. Over the years, teachers and administrators have suggested traits that were not considered in the first study. For example, "apathy" has been characterized by several of them as "Public Enemy #1" in their middle and high schools. Opposites to apathy might be "grit", "desire," and "determination." Also, others have regretted the absence of "fairness." They have not been convinced that it is embedded in "honesty." In any case, for the past decade the 16 traits in Table 2 have been at the core of an evolving character education curriculum (described later and in Hoedel, 2010).

PROCESS TWO: CURRICULUM DEVELOPMENT

Having determined the most desirable character traits to be taught to ninth- through 12th-grade students, the next procedure was to develop lesson plans considered most likely to succeed. The high school principal had already specified the format in his request for help. He wanted a stand-alone, semester-long class focused on character education and leadership. He believed, as did his consultants, that inculcation and nurturing of character traits takes time. Lesson plans were required that made good use of that format.

This task was undertaken by some local members of the Delphi panel, namely, the senior author, the family and child scientist, the high school principal, the two youth ministers, and the director of the mentoring program for at-risk adolescents. They decided that:

1. The key structural elements of the initial curriculum would begin with empirically derived pedagogical practices (so-called "best practices"), namely, the classroom management practices of highly effective high school teachers (e.g., Anderman, Andrzejewski, & Allen, 2011; Berkowitz, 2009; Corso, Bundick, Quaglia, & Haywood, 2013), and experts in efficacious character education (e.g., "what works" by Berkowitz & Bier, 2005; Berkowitz, Bier, & McCauley, 2016; the "four keys" highlighted by Davidson, Fisher, & Lickona, 2009; the "11 principles" designated by character.org, 2010).

2. A consistent and predictable format would be explicitly employed (i.e., students knew what to expect on a daily basis and could prepare for it).

3. Content would be relevant to the students, and focused on specific, realistic, and doable behavioral outcomes.

4. Lesson plans would employ credible and relevant anecdotal illustrations and have students identify role models in their immediate environments. Relevant cultural icons also would be provided.

5. Students would be active learners.

6. Students would be required to interpret, summarize, present, and debate lessons in writing and also in the spoken word. Concurrently their group process would be identified and addressed.

7. The curriculum would be characterized by repetition, multimedia illustrations, and discussion of merits and applications.

8. Teachers would encourage enactment of the lessons learned on campus and in community service.

This pedagogical structure was accepted as fundamental. However, those involved in the program understood that refinement could occur as the number and diversity of participating institutions increased. Therefore, continuous feedback mechanisms were built into their system: Mandated but anonymous written commentary by the students at the conclusion of the term, local and regional meetings with participating teachers and administrators, local and regional trainings and workshops, and— most recently—online blogs and newsletters for all student and adult participants. Based on this feedback the curriculum is now characterized by multifaceted presentations and projects designed to effectively interface with diverse student learning styles. In addition, the program's content and processes were brought into alignment with the English Language Arts (ELA) and English Language Development (ELD) common core standards. This was in response to feedback relative to integration of character education in the overall academic curriculum, as well as awareness of funding opportunities. Recommendations from administrators and teachers most recently resulted in a totally online curriculum. Partly the online version was to address financial nuances and partly to oblige the national push for citizen comfort and competency in the computer age (e.g., Flint, 2014).

Illustration of Curriculum Structure and Its Evolution

Relevant Material in a Consistent and Predictable Format

A consistent format of 10 lesson plans was developed to teach each of the 16 traits, with two more units for consolidation of that which has been learned (180 total lesson plans). This template created a consistent learning environment—everyone in the classroom knew what to expect and when to prepare. Table 3 highlights the 16 traits that were paired with the 16 unit topics, followed by the consolidation units. Table 4 highlights the 10 lesson plans employed to teach each of 18 units.

This structure was put into an evolving teacher's manual (for example, Hoedel, 2012). However, student and teacher feedback indicated that, although most programs were conducted according to the manual, there were others that were not (see *Modes of Implementation* section for what the situation is and how it is being addressed). Therefore the word "unit" meaning a learning module, has replaced "weekly."

Learning Styles

The 10 lesson plans embedded in each unit specifically align with the diverse learning styles of students (see updated review in

TABLE 3
The Topics and Their Associated Traits

18 Unit Topics	Traits of Study
Orientation and Expectations	Attitude
Developing Goals and Priorities	Preparation
The Importance of Education	Perseverance
Showing Respect to Others	Respect
Building a Positive Reputation	Honesty
Developing Personal Values	Integrity
Handling Peer Pressure	Courage
The Importance of Role Models	Appreciation
Managing Anger and Aggression	Composure
Positive Communication Skills	Empathy
Expressing Gratitude to Parents	Gratitude
Cultural Competence	Tolerance
Citizenship in the Community	Service
Sustaining Long-term Relationships	Loyalty
Employability and Workplace Skills	Responsibility
Addressing Bullying in Your School	Compassion
Review and Consolidation	Leadership
Review and Consolidation	Character

Note: Each pair ("unit") is expected to be taught across 18 successive school weeks. The last two pairs are for consolidation of what has been learned.

Moussa, 2014). Increasingly students have considered the concepts of character and leadership through multimedia interactions with the subject matter. There always is didactic, passive learning, such as, lectures about leadership principles. But there also are more active tasks incorporating multiple ways of knowing: Reading (role model readings), writing (writing assignments, blog posts and responses), video presentations (movies exemplifying positive character traits), oral presentations and processing (e.g., small and large group discussion of ethical dilemmas), and exploration of the group process with regard to basic social skills. Finally, as noted above, in 2014 the CD&L curriculum was modified and expanded to instruct students using a 100% online platform (e.g., schools providing indi-

TABLE 4

Ten Consistent Lesson Plans Employed to Teach the 18 Character and Leadership Traits

- **Lesson Plan 1—Quotation Exercise:** This is an informal, low-stress way to introduce the trait and topic. Traits are defined and quotations from both historical and anonymous individuals are provided. Students provide short-answer responses about the context and meaning of the quotations, followed by classroom discussion.

- **Lesson Plan 2—Ethical Dilemma:** Real-life scenarios are used to challenge students to contemplate choices, options, consequences, and different points of view, to help them with critical thinking skills and judgment. Students provide written, short answers and then participate in debate/discussion.

- **Lesson Plan 3—Lecture:** Students receive weekly direct instruction and collaborative question prompts from research-based lectures supported with curriculum-provided Power Points, visuals and handouts.

- **Lesson Plan 4—Character Movies:** Students view, discuss and debate selected scenes from appropriate popular movies that embody the featured character trait. Verbal and/or written responses to follow up questions challenge students to critically analyze these video segments from multiple points of reference.

- **Lesson Plan 5—Role Model Readings:** A textbook has been written which provides the biographies of 17 role models who exemplify each of the 17 traits covered in the curriculum. Each week students read a 10-page biographical narrative about a historical or contemporary person. Chapter quizzes and discussion questions spur in-depth analysis of each featured role model.

- **Lesson Plan 6—Community Role Model:** Understanding that "true" role models resided in the students' community (i.e., lived in the same neighborhoods, graduated from the same schools, and looked like the students), community leaders are brought into the classroom each week to reinforce the importance of the character traits covered in the class. The speakers tell personal stories, provide life lessons, and encourage students to reach their full potential.

- **Lesson Plan 7—Basic Skills:** Practical and essential skills are provided for each module to help students become successful in school and beyond. Almost all of these skills are behavioral in nature, so differences can be observed immediately.

- **Lesson Plan 8—Blog:** An online blog provides a positive, negative, or controversial current event related to character and leadership. An overview and a link to a short news video is provided along with the blogger's (developer, Joe Hoedel) perspective. Follow up discussion questions seek to inspire students to contemplate the importance of character and leadership in today's society.

- **Lesson Plan 9—Leadership Principles:** Virtual lectures on 17 leadership principles are provided on the website by various leaders. Students will learn the key components of timeless leadership, which will help them become successful in school, career and their personal lives. Discussion and social media questions accompany each principle.

- **Lesson Plan 10—Expository Writing Assignment:** Students write expository or persuasive essays about core beliefs and character related issues. This serves as a final academic written assignment that students will present in a formal oral presentation to classmates.

---

vidual laptops allowing virtual and distance learning opportunities).

Alignment With ELA & ELD Common Core Standards

The Common Core Standards have been adopted by most states (cf. Common Core Standards, 2015). Current and potential users of the CD&L Program have observed that its curriculum could be structured to meet both ELA and ELD standards and be integrated into the high school academic curricula. It thereby could serve a dual purpose, namely, teach pro-

social values while improving English proficiency (cf., Character Development & Leadership, 2016a). This dual feature was subsequently achieved for the CD&L Program by a panel of English teachers from a large western state. At the conclusion of a 6-month process, the panel agreed that the CD&L Program supported:

- 80% of the ELA College & Career Readiness Anchor Standards;
- 75% of the 8, 9 & 10 ELA Speaking, Listening, Reading & Writing Standards; and

- 60% of the 11& 12 ELA Speaking, Listening, Reading and Writing Standards.

This alignment has allowed many secondary schools to use the CD&L Program to receive English credit while also getting financial support for it. A one-for-one demonstration of each of the above Core Standards and the CD&L Program's ways of fulfilling it is available at Character Development and Leadership (2016a). A case study of a successful application in an alternative high school setting (Hoedel & Lee, 2017) is summarized below.

Modes of Implementation

The CD&L Program was initially taught as a stand-alone for-credit course on a block (90 minute) schedule. While the "weekly format" hasn't changed, approximately 40% of the 2,000 schools nationwide do not use it in the original manner (Character Development and Leadership Program, 2016b). For example, hundreds of schools use a homeroom format, extending the 180 lesson plans to cover 3 or 4 years of instruction without redundancy. Some choose to integrate this program in already existing classes, such as JROTC, health, physical education, business, and career management. Some schools prefer to focus on seniors, some on at-risk freshmen. Some use it as an elective (e.g., for student body government members). Some schools require their students to take the course as a requirement for graduation. In contrast, some school districts prefer using the CD&L Program in a middle school setting. From its inception schools have had the freedom to choose how to implement the CD&L Program in order to meet their unique goals and objectives. Ironically, while facilitating its acceptance, this freedom of implementation has presented challenges to the developers' mission of empirical development and validation. These program evaluation challenges will be discussed in the final section.

PROCESS THREE: EMPIRICAL VALIDATION OF CURRICULUM

Since 2001, over 2,000 schools from all 50 states have participated in the evolving Character Development and Leadership Program (2015). Many of these have voluntarily participated in process and outcome evaluation, and the results have been used to continuously modify the program. The findings to date are summarized below. This compilation is timely. There may be a sea change occurring in contemporary secondary education. These predicted changes involve diverse online materials and distance learning. Outcome results from the emerging online programs will need to be compared to those based in traditional classrooms.

Although there have been continuous adjustments informed by the experiences of program administrators, institutional staff, and students—such as, replacing individual role models, expanding the videotape library, adding an interactive blog, and adding writing requirements—outcomes assessment has been in place from the beginning (see Hoedel, 2005, 2005).

The original CD&L semester-long class took place in academic years 2001–2003 at a suburban North Carolina high school (http://www.characterandleadership.com/research). A wait-listed comparison group experimental design involving 80 students assessed whether or not participation in the CD&L Program was appealing to these students and associated with improved school attendance, fewer in-school disciplinary occurrences, and higher grade point averages. The attendant student records supported the notion that this was so. Based on these pilot data the CD&L class was promoted at regional education conferences and workshops.

First Formal Outcomes Assessment: North Carolina High Schools

Pursuant to these presentations, the CD&L Program was voluntarily purchased by and implemented in 74 North Carolina high schools in the 2003–2005 academic years. This was fortuitous:

- The North Carolina Legislature in 2001 mandated that every public school in North Carolina develop and implement a plan to teach character education (House Bill 195 - http://www.dpi.state.nc.us/charactereducation/).
- The CD&L lesson plans had been compiled into a manual that these educators could apply immediately (cf., Hoedel, 2012).

Research Questions

There were four research questions. Would students who participated in the CD&L program, unlike those in comparison groups, have better attendance, fewer in-school suspensions, increased grade point averages (GPA), and higher rates of passing the 9th grade End of Course (EOC) Tests administered under the No Child Left Behind Act (see New America Foundation, 2014).

Method

Procedures

All 74 institutions were invited to be a part of this study. To be included in the outcomes assessment, a high school had to contribute one ninth-grade, semester-long class devoted to the CD&L curriculum. Moreover, the teacher of that class had to participate in a one-day on-site training seminar. Finally, the participating high schools had to submit official office data on attendance, suspensions, grade point averages, and passage of the EOC Tests. Most of the schools agreed to these criteria, but only 28 schools (38%) sufficiently followed through. Most agreed to provide comparison groups of "like" freshmen, but only four schools met the requirements for the comparison groups (that is, they provided official office data). Random assignment of the

groups was recommended and sometimes adhered to, but other principals selected teachers they considered "responsible enough" to follow through on the procedures of the study. Therefore, sometimes the homeroom teacher was randomly assigned and sometimes the teacher was selected based on a track record of being "responsible".

Subjects

A total of 825 ninth-grade students completed the semester-long CD&L Program. At that time a semester was 92 instructional days, and the CD&L course was taught daily in a dedicated homeroom setting to approximately 30 students at each school. The corresponding comparison students were enrolled in traditional homerooms wherein the students focused on homework from their core classes. Because both groups derived from the same school settings, the CD&L and comparison students were similar in demographic makeup: Their schools were urban, suburban, or rural, and situated in white and blue collar neighborhoods as well as those characterized by unemployment and poverty. Accordingly, their student populations were socioculturally and socioeconomically diverse. The data in Table 5 demonstrate that, at the start of this study, the CD&L and the comparison groups of students were comparable in their aggregate attendance records, grade point averages, and school disciplinary events.

Results

The data in Table 6 are the "before and after" results for the students in the CD&L and comparison groups. The predata were from these students' school records describing their last semester (last half of the eighth grade). These data then were compared with the same data at the conclusion of the semester in which the CD&L Program was provided. Each block of data was acquired from a 92-instructional-day experience.

TABLE 5

The Comparability of the CD&L Participants (N = 825) and Students in the
Comparison Group (n = 160) at the Beginning of Study According to School Attendance, GPA, and ISS

Measure	*Days Attended*	*n*	*SD*	*t*	*df*	*Significance (1 Tailed)*
CD&L Participants	72.30	825	2.181			
Comparison Group	72.01	160	1.810	2.7	159	Statistically not significant
Measure	GPA					
CD&L Participants	2.10	825	0.720			
Comparison Group	2.40	160	0.459	2.019	159	Statistically not significant
Measure	In school suspensions					
CD&L Participants	1.90	825	1.240			
Comparison Group	1.96	160	1.186	3.256	159	Statistically not significant

Note: The number of instructional days in their school districts was 178 and their GPAs could range between 0.0 and 4.0. *T* tests of the differences between their aggregate averages demonstrate that they are comparable groups.

TABLE 6

Before and After School Attendance, GPA, and ISSs Comparing
CD&L Participants (n = 825) and Students in the Comparison Group (n = 160)

Days Attended	*Before*	*After*	*Sum of Squares*	*df*	*Mean Square*	*F*	*Sig.*
CD&L participants	72.30 (SD = 2.181)	81.25 (SD = 2.575					
Comparison Group	72.01 (SD = 1.810)	72.00 (SD = 1.825)	27.022	1	27.022	5.447	0.049
GPA							
CD&L participants	2.10 (SD = 0.720)	2.60 (SD = 0.450)					
Comparison group	2.40 (SD = 0.459)	2.32 (SD = 0.570)	2.503	1	2.503	9.569	0.002
ISS							
CD&L participants	1.90 (SD = 1.240)	1.0 (SD = 0.800)					
Comparison group	1.96 (SD = 1.186)	2.3 (SD = 1.180)	3.120	1	3.120	5.537	0.049

Note: The number of instructional days in the school district is 178. Grades in classes range from 0.0 to 4.0. Two-way analysis of variance has been employed. Statistical significance (Sig.) is an *F* value < .05.

In that time the group participating in the CD&L course increased their average attendance from 72 days (78%) the previous semester to 81 days (88%) in the just-completed semester. In contrast those students who did not take the CD&L course remained the same (72 days average attendance each semester). Students who took the CD&L course also improved their group's average GPA from 2.1 (for their last 8th grade semester) to 2.6 at the conclusion of their CD&L semester. In contrast, the average GPA of the comparison group, compiled at the same time, decreased from 2.4 to 2.3. Moreover, the students who participated in the CD&L Program averaged only one in-school suspension during that semester, whereas freshmen who did not take the course averaged 2.3 in-school suspensions in that same period of time. Two-way analyses of variance of these data are summarized in Table 6. The improvements in the CD&L students are all statistically significant.

Moreover, although the comparison high schools did not provide these data, CD&L participants bettered their scores on the end of course English and mathematics assessments administered under No Child Left Behind. The previous year, at the end of the 8th grade, only 45% of these students had passed their 8th grade EOC examination in English and only 25% passed their EOC eighth-grade mathematics test. However, at the end of their participation in the CD&L Program, 71% of the students passed their ninth-grade EOC English test and 47% passed their ninth-grade mathematics EOC test.

In addition, on an anonymous survey (see description of the Student Self Report Survey and its revision—SSRS and SSRS-R—below), at the end of their CD&L class, the participants reported that they engaged in less antisocial behavior in their schools (e.g., stealing, bullying, and cheating) and risky behavior (e.g., drinking, smoking, using substances in automobiles) in their communities. They also indicated that they were more optimistic about graduating from high school and going to college. There were no comparison data from the non-CD&L sample.

Discussion

Over a 2-year period, CD&L participants in the ninth grade demonstrated statistically significant improvements (attendance, GPA, and diminution of school disruptive behaviors). A comparison group comprised of ninth graders from the same schools who were not in the CD&L Program did not exhibit these changes. This discovery encouraged the developers of the CD&L Program to extend it to an increasingly wider population of high schools across the country. After all, there has long been concern about the challenging transition from middle school to high school (cf. Habeeb, 2013). Therefore, interventions focused on this educational developmental step seem prudent. However, the biopsychosocial challenges of middle adolescence do not end with completion of the ninth grade (Aprile, 2008). Consequently, developers of the CD&L Program wanted to explore its benefits with students in other grades in diverse high school programs across the nation.

Subsequent Studies Based on the Original Student Self Report Survey (SSRS) and Its Revision (SSRS-R)

The successive national studies are compiled as Table 7. From 2006 to the present date, the number of participating schools and students has exponentially increased. This has been at the expense of no longer obtaining outcome data from student records and a loss of comparison groups. Educational administrators and the teachers assigned to classes wanted neither to meet the obligations of The Family Educational Rights and Privacy Act of 1974 nor the work involved in culling student files. Moreover, teachers with classes of nonparticipating students especially felt disinclined to take on these duties in order to provide untreated comparison groups (lead author, personal observations documented in field notes).

Despite these obstacles perhaps a third of the participating schools had their students complete a standardized self-report survey (SSRS until 2015–2016; SSRS-R thereafter) prior to and at the completion of their CD&L Program. Outcomes were assessed by CD&L's research director. There were 87 items in this self-report. They were taken from those observable behaviors originally provided by the Delphi panel (see Table 2, column three).

In this self-report, students indicated the frequency of undesirable school behaviors (truancy, lateness, cheating, stealing, theft, and substance use). They also indicated the extent to which they were informed by prosocial attitudes and character traits, and engaged in prosocial acts (standing up for a beleaguered student, resisting peer pressure, demonstrations of altruism, and so on).

Finally, the students indicated the extent to which they predicted the learned character traits would be connected to success in their present and future lives, including their academic progress. Review of these self-reports suggested that they were credible. Both the "before" and "after" surveys consistently contained many revelations of substance use, theft, cheating, and bullying. Many students also made very bold disparaging statements about their teachers (e.g.,"He is a dick"), their classmates (e.g., "Some talk too much," "Too much noise and distractions"), the class (e.g., "boring," "worthless," "easy grade"), the textbook (e.g., "boring," "Who cares?"), and their participation (e.g, "It's just something to do during the day"). Overall, although student feedback has been predominantly positive over the years, there always has been a smaller but outspoken chorus of negative voices (about 10%–15% annually).

In 2015 (Lee, 2015b), the SSRS was reevaluated using known group expectations and psychometric assessment of its structure. That is, confirmatory factor analysis assessed the degree to which the SSRS items were assessing the cluster of attitudes and behaviors it was thought to assess. Seven major factors emerged and they clearly involved the hypothesized antisocial and prosocial tendencies:

- antisocial behavior in school (5 survey questions);
- lack of character strength in school and community (6 survey questions);
- optimism about mainstream life goals (9 survey questions);
- demonstration of prosocial character traits (17 survey questions);

- external versus internal causality (5 survey questions);
- exhibition of socioemotional intelligence ("emotional IQ"; 11 survey questions); and
- honestly in pursuit of goals (5 survey questions).

SSRS survey questions that did not significantly contribute to these seven factors and those which were redundant were eliminated. Accordingly the 87 survey questions of the SSRS were reduced to 58. However, five new items thought to assess student resilience were added (e.g., external causality, openness to outside help, affirming belief systems). In addition, 15 "critical items" were added to the post-CD&L Program student self-report. These questions inquired into the incidence of serious behaviors that in the past were infrequently cited but the presence or absence of which might be of interest to school administrators. Ten of these questions had to do with unsafe behaviors on the part of the respondents over the course of the semester (e.g., their use of illicit substances, drunk driving). Five other questions inquired into student security (e.g., incidence of robbery, assault, and so on,). The revised survey (SSRS-R) is given as an appendix.

Annual or biennial research outcome studies based on these student surveys were completed by CD&L personnel and given to the participating schools as technical reports (see Table 7: Weikert, 2008, 2009, 2010; Lee, 2014a, 2015a, 2016). CD&L Programs in each of these years uniformly obtained statistically significant decreases in undesirable behaviors and increases in prosocial behavior and attitudes. For example, in the 2009–2010 academic year all four antisocial clusters and two of 5 prosocial clusters were statistically significant pre- and post-CD&L Program (for details, see Table 7). Concurrently, with the exception of a few outliers, participating students have overwhelmingly placed the CD&L Program in the top tier of their high school academic experiences with regard to interest and influence.

TABLE 7
Summary of CD&L Program Outcomes Research from 2006 through 1015

Academic Years	Author	Participants	Statistically Significant Changes Associated With CD&L Participation ($p < .05$, One-Tailed Tests)
2006–2008	Weikert	2,632 male and female 9th–12th graders from 72 schools	Significant positive self-reported changes in 3 of 4 antisocial and 3 of 5 prosocial clusters of attitudes and behaviors.
2009–2010	Weikert	1,344 male and female 9th–12th graders from 34 high schools	Significant positive self-reported changes in all 4 antisocial and 2 of 5 prosocial clusters of attitudes and behaviors.
2012–2014	Lee	1,574 9th–12th male and female students from 34 schools	Significant decrease in absences, tardies, fights, and suspensions. Overall positive changes in prosocial attitude and behaviors but not evenly across the expected clusters.
2014–2015	Lee	999 male and female 9th–12th graders from 32 schools	Significant decreases in all 6 antisocial school behaviors: absences, tardies, theft, fights, suspensions, and cheating; and plagiarism; Moderate increase in all prosocial behaviors, such as, demonstrations of positive values, "Emotional IQ," and optimism in pursuit of mainstream goals.
2015–2016	Lee	3,232 male and female middle and high school students from 27 schools	Significant decreases in not following school rules, fighting, in-school suspensions, cheating and plagiarism, theft, and bullying. Statistically insignificant positive shifts in prosocial attitudes and behaviors.

Note: Each study compared self reports submitted anonymously by high school students at the beginning and at the conclusion of their CDL classes. There were no comparison groups.

Because there were no comparison groups, the CD&L Program students' self-described changes in their attitudes and behaviors could not be firmly attributed to the specifics of CD&L Program participation. After all, the students were 6 months older at the end of their CD&L participation and some changes could be the result of developmental maturation. It also is possible that the positive changes were not related to the program content, but occurred because the students were being observed, had volunteered, experienced nonassessed environmental changes, and so on (see Podsokoff, MacKenzie, & Podsakoff, 2012).

Assessing the Results of Using the CD&L Program to Meet Common Core English Language Standards

In a case study described elsewhere (Hoedel & Lee, 2017), the Character Develop-ment and Leadership program replaced an alternative high school's traditional English language offerings. A nontreated comparison group of students who were enrolled in the high school the academic year previous to the use of the CD&L Program were compared to the students who entered the high school the year the CD&L Program was initiated and the year following. Those students who participated in the CD&L Program attended more days (see Figure 2) and passed more courses each semester with higher grade point averages. For more extensive data, including prosocial attitudinal and behavioral advances, the readers are referred to the actual publication.

Discussion: Progress, Limitations, and Lessons Learned

The three studies with comparison samples —pilot, North Carolina Schools, alternative education—demonstrate that the CD&L Program is associated with discernible diminution of antisocial behaviors and advances in prosocial behavior and attitudes in schools and communities. Moreover, all the outcome studies that have been based only on student self-reports before and at the end of the CD&L program—in the absence of comparison groups—also support the benefits of such a program. Moreover, most participating students have regarded the CD&L Program enthusiastically, both in terms of capturing their interest and influencing them in a positive manner.

Choosing to intervene directly with students in specialized classrooms is mildly at odds with contemporary thinking in character education (cf. Berkowitz, Battistich, & Bier, 2008; Berkowitz & Bier, 2005). The overriding theoretical orientation has been that it is the school's culture which results in substantive sustained change in its students (cf. reviews and discussions in Berkowitz & Bier, 2005; character.org, 2010; Josephson, 2015; Levingston, 2009; Lickona, 1992, Lickona & Davidson, 2005; Liston, 2014; Mackenzie & Mackenzie, 2010). Nevertheless, over a decade ago Berkowitz and Bier (2004, 2007) observed that character education in the schools often had not been research driven and empirically assessed. They then listed interventions that had been empirically based. But only two interventions addressed high school students (Berkowitz & Bier, 2007). Moreover, neither of these had explored the efficacy of continuous lesson-based interventions in the classroom, that is, specialized classes lasting a full semester or longer. This paper suggests that this may be an additional way to improve the character of students and the climate of a school.

Nevertheless, it is important to appreciate that the entire program of study detailed in this paper has taken place "in the trenches" and not in sophisticated institutional research settings. Therefore, there are limitations in the CD&L Program outcome studies and what has allegedly been discovered to date. These limitations involve:

- **Evaluation of a dynamic developmental process.** Since 2001, over 2,000 schools from all 50 states have participated in the evolving Character Development and Leadership Program (2015), but not all at the same time. Almost all of these schools voluntarily participated in process and outcome evaluation, and the results have been used to continuously modify the program. For example, a textbook of role model biographies was added in 2004 and, from 2005 to 2012, some role models were dropped and new ones added so that they remained relevant to the additional cohorts of students. For the same reason the library of recommended character movies—one per unit—has been continually updated. Technological advances also allowed the development of an interactive online blog, replete with updated videotaped vignettes which allow the students to analyze current events related to character and leadership. This blog gives the teacher a weekly lesson plan that is always current and relevant. Finally, with the advent of the Common Core, emphasis was placed on aligning the CD&L classes with the common core standards for English, which placed an emphasis on speaking, listening, reading and writing. In particular, students were required to write weekly expository papers on their core beliefs and "big picture" ideas and then to provide oral presentations using good public speaking skills in front of their CD&L peers. These ongoing changes have been prompted and shaped though feedback from students, teachers, and the anonymous written critiques and suggestions at the end of their programs by the students. Because these changes were incorporated for the CD&L Program as a whole at the beginning of each academic year, each year should be appreciated in its own right. With a program in flux, out in the field, one looks for signs of continuous desirable outcomes.

- *Two thirds of the outcomes assessments rely on student self-reports.* Having the students assess themselves will always be crucial. These surveys indicate the extent to which the students believe that they are internalizing prosocial traits. Their self-reports have shown remarkable candor (e.g., admission of substance use, cheating and plagiarism, etc.). Nevertheless, outcome assessment needs to consistently include academic and disciplinary records in order to determine to what extent the participants' actual behavior matches their professed beliefs as well as the short-term behavioral outcomes desired by teachers and administrators. Aggregate culling and analysis of school records will preserve the students' right to privacy.

- *Two thirds of the outcomes assessments do not employ comparison groups.* Attributions of positive outcomes can only be strictly attributable to the CD&L Program if well-conceived comparison groups are used. Otherwise, there is no way to know if prosocial attitudes and behavior have resulted from normal maturation influenced by the sociocultural context of their school (cf., Ford & Lerner, 1992), or by the special attention students have received during the course of this program.

- **Program fidelity has been an ongoing challenge.** Although there is an operations manual (Hoedel, 2012) and a training on DVD, how best to implement the CD&L program often has been left to the consumers—those "in the trenches"—to decide how to best implement it based on their resources, priorities, and objectives. Consequently, schools have implemented the CD&L

curriculum in a variety of highly nuanced ways. This flexibility may have helped schools become more successful with this program, but it has also made the results of efficacy studies more nebulous. The problem is that attributing outcomes to a manualized program can only be as valid as its users follow the dictates of the operations manual. Interested parties must be assured that those who are allegedly using this curriculum are rigorously trained using the operations manual, and that they faithfully follow its instructions. This so-called "program fidelity" is sustained by continuing oversight of how the program is being administered and program-long feedback between developers and users. (See Lee, 2014b, for a detailed discussion of this matter.)

- **The sustainability of perceived changes.** Finally, how does one know that the changes thought to be produced by the CD&L Program continue after participation is over? Longitudinal studies are needed both in the school context (for example, ninth graders' success in their remaining high school years) and in the postgraduation and young adult era. Such studies also hold the promise of illuminating what ecosystemic variables influence positive and negative characterological challenges and resources during these important developmental eras. (See discussions and methodologies offered by Lerner & Callina, 2014; VanLaningham, Johnson, & Amato, 2001).

CONCLUSION

In a direct response to a community request the CD&L Program has spent the past 15 years ascertaining the extent to which a high dosage, well-conceived, and consistent character education curriculum for high school students in a dedicated classroom can change students' lives in the school setting. The school principal who first requested this program assumed that, if a cohesive, comprehensive, sequenced course of study moved students in a prosocial direction, the social systems (classrooms and campus) of which they were a living part would also become more prosocial. The school would get cadres of leaders and mentors to instigate, celebrate, and support positive social growth in the student body.

This article narrates the logical first steps in evolving a program of scientifically based pedagogy. It has employed best empirical practices to achieve consensus about what character traits should be cultivated in focused classrooms for contemporary ninth through 12th graders for mainstream success. It has acquired a somewhat uneven but consistent program of outcome determination. It has created and sustained a continuous feedback loop between program developers, evaluators, and consumers. The mission remains ongoing, to wit, the evolution of a character education program for middle adolescents in their schools that not only is student-friendly but also is informed both by theory and empirical data.

REFERENCES

Anderman, L., Andrzejewski, C. E., & Allen, J. (2011). How do teachers support students' motivation and learning in their classrooms? *Teachers College Record, 113*, 963–1003.

Aprile, D. (2008). *Using piecewise growth modeling to understand urban youth's experiences of the transition to high school.* ProQuest Information & Learning (AAI3299568).

Berkowitz, M. W. (2009). Teaching in your prime: The fab five of educating for learning and character. In D. Straight (Ed.). *Good things to do: Expert suggestions for fostering goodness in kids* (pp. 9–14). Portland OR: The Council for Spiritual and Ethical Education.

Berkowitz, M. W., Battistich, V., & Bier, M. C. (2008). What works in character education: What is known and needs to be known? In L. P. Nucci & D. Nervaez (Eds.), *Handbook of moral and character education* (pp. 414–431). New York, Routledge.

Berkowitz, M. W., & Bier, M. C. (2004). Research-based character education. *Annals of the American Academy of Political and Social Science, 59*, 72–85.

Berkowitz, M. W., & Bier, M. C. (2005). *What works in character education: A report for policy makers and opinion leaders.* Washington DC: Character Education Partnership.

Berkowitz, M. W., & Bier, M. C. (2007). What works in character education. *Journal of Research in Character Education, 5*, 29–48.

Berkowitz, M. W., Bier, M. C., & McCauley, B. (2016, July). *Effective features and practices that support character development.* Paper presented at the National Academies of Sciences, Engineering, and Medicine Workshop on Defining and Measuring Character and Character Education, Washington, DC.

Character Development and Leadership Program (2015). *Changing students! Changing schools! Changing communities!* Retrieved March 4, 2015, from http://www.characterandleadership .com

Character Development and Leadership. (2016a). How we meet the new ELA Common Core Standards. Retrieved 02/21/2016 from http://www.characterandleadership.com

Character Development and Leadership. (2016b). A Proven character education and leadership curriculum for high schools and middle schools. Retrieved February 21, 2016, from http://www.characterandleadership.com

character.org. (2010). *The eleven principles of effective character education: A framework for school success.* Washington, DC: Author.

Common Core Standard. (2015). Retrieved from http://www.commoncorestandards.org

Corso, M. F., Bundick, M. J., Quaglia, R. J., & Haywood, D. (2013). Where student, teacher, and content meet: Student engagement in the secondary school classroom. *American Secondary Education, 41*(3), 50–61.

David, H.A. (1988). *The method of paired comparisons.* New York, NY: Oxford University Press.

Davidson, M. (2004). *Developing performance character and moral character in youth. The fourth and fifth Rs: Respect and Responsibility. 10* (2). Retrieved from http://www.cortland.edu/ c4n5rs

Davidson, M., Fisher, C., & Lickona, T. (2009, Winter). The 4 keys: Maximizing the power of any chapter educate practice. *Excellence & Ethics,* 1–4.

Davidson, M., Lickona, T., & Kmelkov, V. (2008). Smart and good schools: A new paradigm for high school character education. In L. P. Nucci & D. Nervaez (Eds.), *Handbook of moral and character education* (pp. 370–390). New York, NY: Taylor & Francis.

Dick, B. (2000). *A beginner's guide to action research.* Available at http://www.uq.net.au/action_research/arp/guide.html

Fedson, D. S. (1998). Efficacy versus effectiveness. *Developments in Biological Standardization, 95,* 195–201.

Fletcher, A. J., & Marchildon, G. P. (2011). Using the Delphi method for qualitative, participatory action research in health leadership. *International Journal of Qualitative Methods, 13,* 1–18.

Flint, K. (2014). Obama becomes first president to write a computer program. Retrieved February 21, 2016, from http://www.wired.com/2014/12/obama-becomes-first-president-write-computer-program/

Ford, D. H., & Lerner, R. M., (1992) *Developmental systems theory: An integrative approach.* Thousand Oaks, CA: SAGE.

Fraenkel, J., Wallen, N., & Hyun, H. (2011). *How to design and evaluate research in education* (8th ed.). New York, NY: McGraw-Hill.

Godwin, M., Ruhland, L., Casson, I., Mcdonald, S., Delva, D., Birtwhistle, R., Lam, M., & Seguin, R. (2003). Pragmatic controlled clinical trials in primary care: The struggle between external and internal validity. *BioMedCentral Medical Research Methodology, 10,* 3–28.

Green, K. C., Armstrong, J.S., & Graefe, A. (2007). Methods to elicit forecasts from groups: Delphi and prediction markets compared. *Foresight: The International Journal of Applied Forecasting, 8,* 17–20.

Habeeb, S. (2013). The ninth-grade challenge. *Principal Leadership, 13*(6), 18–22.

Helmer-Hirschberg, O. (1966). *The use of Delphi technique in problems of educational innovations.* Santa Monica, CA: Rand Corporation.

Hoedel, J. M. (2005). *A study of select schools using the Character Development and Leadership Curriculum.* Greensboro, NC: Character and Leadership Development Program.

Hoedel, J. (2010). *Character & leadership development: A proven curriculum.* Retrieved from http://www.characterandleadership.com

Hoedel, J. M. (2012). *Character development & leadership: Role models edition.* Williamsburg, MI: Character Development & Leadership - Skills That Last a Life-time.

Hoedel, J. M., & Lee, R. E. (2017). Meeting Common Core English Language Arts and English Language Development standards with character education lesson plans in alternative education Grades 9 though 12. *Journal of Character Education, Volume 12*(1), pp. 1–14.

Josephson, M. (2015). *Six pillars of character* Retrieved from http://josephsoninstitute.org/sixpillars.html

Lee, R. E. (2014a). *A quantitative and qualitative study of select schools using the Character Development and Leadership Curriculum: All-schools report.* Williamsburg, MI: Character and Leadership Development Program.

Lee, R. E. (2014b). Tools: Supervising manual-based models. In R. E. Lee & Thorana S. Nelson, *The contemporary relational supervisor* (pp. 111–116). New York, NY: Routledge.

Lee, R. E. (2015a). *A quantitative and qualitative study of select schools using the Character Development and Leadership Curriculum: All-schools report.* Williamsburg, MI: Character and Leadership Development Program.

Lee, R. E. (2015b). *The CD&L Program Student Self-Report (SSRS): Psychometric evaluation and revision* (Technical report). Williamsburg, MI: Character and Leadership Development Program.

Lee, R. E. (2016). *A quantitative and qualitative study of select schools using the Character Development and Leadership Curriculum: All-schools report.* Williamsburg, MI: Character and Leadership Development Program.

Lerner, R. M., & Callina, K. S. (2014). The study of character development: Towards tests of a relational developmental systems model. *Human Development, 57,* 322–346.

Levingston, J. K. (2009). *Sowing the seeds of character: The moral education of adolescents in public and private schools.* Santa Barbara, CA: Praeger.

Lickona, T. (1992). *Educating for character: How our schools can teach respect and responsibility.* New York, NY: Bantam.

Lickona, T., & Davidson, M. (2005). *A report to the Nation: Smart & good high schools. Integrating excellence and ethics for success in school, work, and beyond.* Washington, DC: Character Education Partnership.

Liston, M. (2014). *Executive summary: Conceptualizing and validating the Character Growth Index*

(CGI). Retrieved September 20, 2015, ProQuest Information and Learning (A13633828).

Mackenzie, S. V., & Mackenzie, G. C. (2010). *Now what? Confronting and resolving ethical questions: A handbook for teachers.* Thousand Oaks, CA: Corwin/SAGE.

Moussa, N. M. (2014). The importance of learning styles in education. *Institute for Learning Styles Journal, 1,* 19–27.

New America Foundation. (2014). *No child left behind: Overview.* Retrieved March 5, 2015, from http://febp.newamerica.net/background-analysis/no-child-left-behind-overview

Podsakoff, P. M., MacKenzie, S. B., & Podsakoff, N. P. (2012). Sources of method bias in social science research and recommendations on how to comparison it. *Annual Review of Psychology, 63,* 539–569.

Turoff, M., & Linstone, H. (Eds.). (2002). *The Delphi method: Methods and applications.* Retrieved from http://is.njit.edu/pubs/delphibook/delphibook.pdf

VanLaningham, J., Johnson D. R., & Amato, P. (2001). Marital happiness, marital duration, and the U-shaped curve: Evidence from a five-wave panel study. *Social Forces, 79,* 1313–1341.

Weikert, P. S. (2008). *A quantitative and qualitative study of select schools using the Character Development and Leadership Curriculum: All-schools report.* Williamsburg, MI: Character and Leadership Development Program.

Weikert, P. S. (2009). *A quantitative and qualitative study of select schools using the Character Development and Leadership Curriculum: All-schools report.* Williamsburg, MI: Character and Leadership Development Program.

Weikert, P. S. (2010). *A quantitative and qualitative study of select schools using the Character Development and Leadership Curriculum: All-schools report.* Williamsburg, MI: Character and Leadership Development Program.

APPENDIX: THE REVISED STUDENT SELF REPORT SURVEY (SSRS-R)

Post-program Survey	
Date Year	20___
Semester	Fall (1) — Spring (2)
My grade	6th through 8th — 9 -- 10 --11-12
My teacher is	Alphanumeric
My gender is	female 1, male 2
I consider myself	Native American (1) - Black (2) —Asian(3) ——Hispanic (4) ——White (5) ——Mixed Race (6)
I 'm taking this class because	I signed up for this elective (1) — I was told I had to (2) — This is part of my Homeroom/Advisory period (3) — It's required for graduation (4)
I am looking forward to this class	No (1) — I don't care (2) — Yes (3),

UNDESIRABLE ATTRIBUTES	
Antisocial behavior in school	-11 questions-
About how many times did the following things happen this semester?	"I got in trouble for not following school rules"
(5 questions)	"I was put on an in-school suspension"
About once a week (1) About once a month (2) 2 or 3 times last semester (3) 1 time last semester (4) Never (5)	"I was suspended or put on probation from school"
	"My parents received a warning from school"
	"I got into a physical fight at school"
Lack of character strength in school and community	
About how many times did the following things happen this semester?	"I cheated on an exam"
(6 questions)	"I plagiarized or shared answers on a homework assignment"
About once a week (1) About once a month (2) 2 or 3 times last semester (3) 1 time last semester (4) Never (5)	"I stole something from a store, friend, or relative"
	"I lied to a friend or relative"
	"I picked on another student"
	"I gave into peer pressure when I knew I shouldn't have"

DESIRABLE ATTRIBUTES	
Optimism about mainstream life goals	-48 questions-
Think about the future. How sure are you?	"I will graduate from high school"
(9 questions)	"I will go to college"
I don't believe it (1) I have much doubt (2) I believe it could happen (3) I am pretty sure it will happen (4) I am convinced of it (5)	"I will have a job that pays well"
	"I will have a job that I enjoy doing"
	"I will have a happy family life"
	"I will be respected in my community"
	"I will have good friends I can count on"
	"Life will turn out better for me than it has for my parents"
Mainstream prosocial values	
How often this semester do you demonstrate each of the following traits?	Positive attitude
(17 questions)	Preparation
Always (1) Often (2) Occasionally (3) Rarely (4) Never (5)	Perseverence
	Respect
	Honesty
	Integrity
	Courage
	Appreciation
	Composure; self control of anger and behavior
	Empathy
	Gratitude
	Tolerance
	Sacrifice
	Loyalty
	Responsibility
	Compassion
	Leadership
Internal Causality	
As things are right now, how convinced are you?	"The traits listed in the this 17 questions are important for my future success"
(5 questions)	"My decisions and hard work will make me successful!"
Highly disagree (1) Somewhat disagree (2) I don't know (3) Somewhat agree (4) Agree very much (5)	"I know how to set goals to get important things done"
	"I shouldn't put off things that need doing"
	"I know how to get help from others if I need it"

Demonstrates socio-emotional intelligence	
This semester:	"I put in extra time, effort, and/or did extra credit work in order to get a better grade"
(11 questions)	"I went out of my way to help another student"
Never (1) Rarely (2) Sometimes (3) Many times (4) Always (5)	"I worked hard to resolve a problem with a teacher"
	"I worked hard to resolve a problem with a classmate"
	"I intervened to help someone who was getting picked on"
	"When I was stressed or mad I still made good decisions"
	"I let a classmate know his/her behavior was inappropriate"
	"I told a parent or role model how much I appreciated them"
	"I chose the right way over the easy way"
	"I demonstrated positive leadership skills"
Honesty in pursuit of goals	
In my life, right now, I believe	"I would not lie to get a job"
(5 questions)	"I don't have to lie or cheat in order to succeed"
Highly disagree (1) Somewhat disagree (2) I don't know (3) Somewhat agree (4) Agree very much (5)	"When it comes to doing what is right I am better than most people I know"
	"It is important to me that people trust me"
	"It is not worth it to lie or cheat because it hurts my character"
Critical Items (rare but urgent), or not differentiating, or low loading on components. (15 questions added to above)	
Formal altruistic investment *In the this semester*	"I was involved in community service" Never (1) Once (2) More than once (3)
Rare negative incidents	More than once (1) Once (2) Never (3)
	"I was arrested "
	"I drove when I had been drinking alcohol or was high"
	"I rode in a car when the driver had been drinking or was high"
	"I drank alcohol"
	"I smoked cigarettes or used chewing tobacco or snuff"
	"I used marijuana"
	"I used other street and recreational drugs"
	"I cut classes"
"Student victimization": Campus climate	
(Only relevant to extent that most students are enrolled) *This semester:*	"I was bullied by someone on school property"
	"I had something stolen from me at school"
	"Someone verbally threatened to hurt me at school"
	"Someone threatened me with a weapon on school property"
	"Someone at school offered to sell me drugs"
Student Feedback	
Would you recommend this class to a friend?	No (1) ---- Maybe (2) ---- Yes (3).
Please explain your answer	text
How much influence did this class have on you?	None (1) Some (2) A lot (3)
Please explain your answer	text
What would make this class better?	text

CHARACTER EDUCATION IN HIGH SCHOOL ATHLETICS
Perspectives From Athletics Directors on a Curriculum to Promote Character Development Through Sport

Andrea Vest Ettekal
Texas A&M University

Brian Burkhard
Tufts University

Kaitlyn A. Ferris
University of Chicago

Kristina L. Moore
Boston College

Richard M. Lerner
Tufts University

Given the ubiquity of youth sport, it has the potential to impact character development among millions of American youth. However, findings about the youth sport-character development relation have been mixed. Character education may be necessary to optimize the sport environment to promote character attributes. There is much knowledge of what works in character education within schools, but less is known about character education in interscholastic sports. In this study, we examined athletics directors' (ADs) perspectives of a sport-based character education program from Positive Coaching Alliance (PCA) implemented through their high school athletics departments. ADs discussed factors that mattered for implementing PCA programming, as well as perceived effects of PCA programming among their high school coaches and athletes. Our discussion integrates findings from this study with previous knowledge about effective character education programs in schools. With the goal of using ADs as informants who have expertise in interscholastic sport, findings from this study generated new hypotheses to be tested in future studies to further understanding of character education in sport.

About 70% of American youth participated in school- or community-based sports in recent years (Holt, 2016; Sabo & Veliz, 2008; Vandell, Larson, Mahoney, & Watts, 2015). Sport is discussed as a setting to promote positive youth development (Holt, 2016). However, whether sport promotes character is controversial, such that some findings suggest that sport

• **Correspondence concerning this article should be addressed to:** Andrea Vest Ettekal, andrea.ettekal@tamu.edu

Journal of Character Education, Volume 14(1), 2018, pp. 29–43
ISSN 1543-1223

participation promotes character attributes, whereas others suggest the contrary (Bredemeier & Shields, 2006; Rudd, 2005). Mixed findings about the sport-character development relation may be largely due to the wide variation in the quality of sport programs.

Previous research overwhelmingly supports that high quality youth development programs promote the most positive youth outcomes (e.g., Yohalem, Wilson-Ahlstrom, Fischer, & Shinn, 2007). Universal features of high quality youth development programs include having a safe physical environment, as well as the presence of supportive relationships and positive social norms, to name a few (e.g., Eccles & Gootman, 2002). However, intentional efforts are necessary to ensure youth development programs are high quality. Thus, explicit curricula may be necessary to promote high quality sport programs, such as by promoting positive coaching behaviors, addressing conceptions of competition, and providing opportunities for character development (Bredemeier & Shields, 1986, 2006). In this study, we examine athletics directors' (ADs) perspectives on the effectiveness of a sport-based character education program from Positive Coaching Alliance (PCA).

There is much knowledge of "what works" in character education in schools (Berkowitz, Bier, & McCauley, 2017), but less is known about character education in sport. In high school interscholastic sports, ADs have a significant influence on the goals, vision, and mission of the athletics programs. Thus, we conducted a focus group with ADs after they had engaged in PCA's character education program implemented through their high school athletics departments. Accordingly, in this hypothesis-searching study (Cattell, 1966), the ADs served as a panel of informants who have been judged by school administrators to have sufficient expertise in interscholastic sport to be hired into positions of leadership of these programs. Our goal was to integrate the views of ADs who experienced PCA programming with what is known about effective character education in schools to present hypotheses about effective sport-based character education.

Character Development in Achievement Contexts: The Case for Sport

Given the plethora of knowledge of what works in character education in schools (Berkowitz & Bier, 2014), classroom settings might serve as a starting point for understanding character education through interscholastic sport. Sport is similar to classrooms because they are both achievement settings that provide opportunities for youth to develop competence (Duda & Nicholls, 1992). What distinguishes sport from the classroom is that participation is voluntary and occurs outside of the traditional school curriculum. Sport also differs from school because of the central focus on competition (Bredemeier & Shields, 1986). Sport by definition involves participating in a game in which there are winners and losers (Shields & Bredemeier, 2011).

The game component of sport matters considerably for youth character development. According to game reasoning theory (Bredemeier & Shields, 1986), some youth compromise moral principles and prioritize performance goals (e.g., winning) over mastery goals (e.g., personal improvement) because the game is not "real life." In other words, some youth athletes engage in behaviors during sport that they know are not moral (e.g. intentionally injuring an opponent), but not in settings outside of sport. Thus, sport has the potential to promote or inhibit athletes' character. We wish to elucidate ideas pertinent to the process through which the potential to promote character is instantiated by engaging with sport-based character education.

Character Education in Sport: What Works?

Positive youth development involves mutually beneficial exchanges between individuals and their environments, termed individual ⇔ context relations (Lerner, Lerner, Bowers, &

Geldhof, 2015). Character development involves individuals positively engaging with their social world (Nucci, 2001, 2017). Thus, extending the positive youth development perspective, character development involves mutually beneficial individual ⇔ relations but, more specifically, positive individual ⇔ individual relations (Lerner & Callina, 2014). There are a variety of curricula to promote youth character development and many of them are situated within schools (Berkowitz & Bier, 2014). The most effective character education strategies are summarized in Berkowitz and colleagues' PRIMED model (Berkowitz et al., 2017). According to the PRIMED model, character education must be Prioritized in the (educational) setting; Relationships should be proactively and strategically nurtured; Intrinsic motivation should be the primary motivational aim; Models of character should be readily available to students; stakeholders should be Empowered and supported; and the curriculum should be Developmentally appropriate. Together, the strategies in the PRIMED model represent optimal character education implementation (Berkowitz et al., 2017).

A widely used sport-based character education curriculum was developed by PCA, a national nonprofit focused on promoting character through youth sport (Thompson, 2010). Specifically, PCA's mission is to "transform the youth sports culture into a *development zone* where all youth and high school athletes have a positive, character-building experience that results in Better Athletes, Better People" (www.positivecoach.org). PCA uses a partnership model to form relationships with athletics programs and jointly implement the curriculum with coaches and youth athletes. The PCA theory of change states that if (1) coaches and athletes engage with PCA programming; then (2) coaches will become double-goal coaches who focus on winning *and* life lessons, and athletes will become triple impact competitors who focus on contributing to a better self, better teammates, and a better game; and in turn, (3) athletes will contribute positively to society. PCA programming involves coaches and athletes participating in separate 60- to 90-minute workshops, which highlight principles to promote athletes' character development, reading a book about PCA principles of character, and coaches and athletes engaging in weekly talking points about specific character-focused scenarios in sport. The purpose of this study was to use PCA as an example case to generate expertise-informed (AD-informed) hypotheses for future studies (Cattell, 1966) that could enhance our understanding of the processes involved in successful sport-based character education.

In theory, PCA's mission and curriculum align with the PRIMED model of character education. First, PCA's mission of developing double-goal coaches is to encourage coaches to *Prioritize* the development of character attributes (i.e., life lessons) alongside the goal of winning. Second, nurturing *relationships* is crucial for PCA, such that the coach-athlete relationship is central to fostering character development in young people through the sport context. Moreover, PCA provides tools (e.g., talking points) to support coach facilitation of positive communication about character virtues with athletes. Third, PCA's approach is to allow extrinsic motivations, such as an emphasis on performance goals (e.g., winning), but to simultaneously elevate *Intrinsic* motivations (e.g., personal improvements) to be of equal emphasis within the sport arena. Fourth, to achieve their mission and goals, PCA trains administrators, coaches, and parents to be positive and approachable *models* of character. Fifth, PCA seeks to *empower* stakeholders by giving ADs, parents, and coaches a voice in determining the focus of curriculum content. Finally, PCA provides *developmentally* appropriate curricula by tailoring their curriculum content and delivery approaches depending on the particular set of youth athletes who participate in particular sports. In this study, we examine the alignment between ADs' perspectives of how PCA was delivered in practice and the elements of the PRIMED model.

Summary and Study Goals

To our knowledge, there are few, theory-guided studies of sport-based character education. We used qualitative methods to explore ADs' perspectives after engaging with PCA programming in their high school athletics programs. Understanding ADs' perspectives of PCA programming provides a starting point for generating hypotheses about processes involved in sport-based character education. Our hope was that this "hypothesis seeking" study (Cattell, 1966) will generate new hypotheses about the process of sport-based character education to be tested in future studies.

METHOD

This study was part of a larger evaluation of PCA (Ettekal, Konowitz, Agans, Syer, & Lerner, 2017). The larger evaluation, which took place from the fall of 2014 until the spring of 2017, involved a longitudinal examination of youth athletes' character attributes. Prior to fall 2014, the ADs at four Boston area high schools were approached by a staff member from PCA and offered free PCA programming in return for participating in a research study. The ADs had no prior experience with character education programs. Utilizing a waitlist control design (Maholmes & Lomonaco, 2010), two schools received PCA programming during the first year, whereas the other two schools waited to receive PCA programming until the second year; all four schools received PCA programming during the third and final year. The ADs were not originally enrolled as participants in the study, but helped the researchers coordinate recruitment and enrollment of athletes and coaches from their high schools. ADs also helped PCA implement the curriculum (e.g., scheduling PCA workshops). At the time of the focus group, the results of the larger evaluation study (i.e., whether PCA promoted athletes' character development) were not yet revealed.

Participants

We briefly describe the demographics of the ADs and schools, but some details are excluded to maintain anonymity. There were four ADs (both genders represented), each with at least five years of experience as an AD. We refer to the ADs using the following pseudonyms: Devon, Alex, Jordan, and Avery. All four ADs had graduate degrees in either educational or athletics administration. The four ADs were about the same age (mid-30s to mid-40s). The four high schools each served ninth through twelfth grade and were in the Boston-area suburbs. Two of the schools had mostly White students (i.e., >75%), whereas two of the schools had students who were ethnically diverse (i.e., 60% Black and 40% Hispanic youth). The four high schools varied in size with 697–1,686 students enrolled. We purposefully do not identify which ADs belonged to which schools to maintain anonymity.

Procedures

In the fall of 2016, the ADs were invited to participate in a focus group about their experiences with PCA programming. The focus group took place at a public restaurant during the day and was audio-recorded for later transcription and analysis. There were two researchers present to moderate the focus group using a semistructured interview guide. The two researchers had been involved in the larger evaluation study from the outset and maintained positive relationships with the ADs throughout the study. The researchers were understood by the ADs and student-athletes to be separate entities from PCA (i.e., not representatives or employees of PCA) by verbally declaring their representation as their university affiliation and by wearing university-affiliated attire during their interactions. The interview format was divided into four sections: (1). What do you think about character development through sport?; (2) Do you value PCA's mission?; (3) How did you implement

PCA in your school?; and (4) Did you perceive any changes among your coaches and athletes as a result of participating in PCA programming? The focus group lasted approximately two hours and each AD received a gift card for his/her participation.

Analysis Plan

The research team used a combination of deductive and inductive approaches (Thomas, 2006). The team conducted a qualitative content analysis (Hsieh & Shannon, 2005) with primary and secondary data coding (Ryan & Bernard, 2003). The analysis was led primarily by the first and second authors of this paper, but all authors were involved in interpretation and resolving discrepancies. Data coding proceeded in several steps. First, three of the authors read the entire transcript and took notes on major themes. The themes identified during note-taking loosely corresponded with the four primary sections of the interview. The first and second author each coded the entire transcript for the primary themes in Microsoft Word using the comment function in track changes. The authors revised the primary coding until they were in 100% agreement. Second, the first and second authors read each of the primary themes and wrote memos for emergent secondary themes (Emerson, Fretz, & Shaw, 1995). After deciding on secondary themes, the first author coded all excerpts and a reliability check was conducted on 20% of the excerpts by the second author. Team members wrote integrative memos of their reflections on codes and relations among the codes during the entire coding process (Emerson et al., 1995). Finally, the researchers created data displays in Microsoft Excel to examine patterns of topics that emerged (Miles & Huberman, 1994).

RESULTS

As shown in Figure 1, the focus group unveiled six primary themes. Three of the themes were deductive, including the decision to engage in PCA programming (Box 1 in Figure 1), how PCA programming was implemented (Box 2 in Figure 1), and whether there were any perceived effects of PCA programming (Box 3 in Figure 1). Two themes were inductive, including factors that mattered for how well the program was implemented (Box A in Figure 1), and factors that might promote or inhibit the effectiveness of PCA programming (Box B in Figure 1). The Boxes labeled "A" and "B" are shown in the figure as potential *conceptual* mediators or moderators that could be tested analytically in future studies.

Deciding to Engage With Character Education

As shown in Figure 1 (Box 1), the first step was deciding to use PCA programming. Three factors mattered for the decision to use PCA programming, including ADs' beliefs about character, ADs' motivational locus, and funding availability. First, all ADs expressed positive beliefs about character suggesting that character development "is important" or that character is "a part of sport." The attributes used to encapsulate character in sport included "respect," "pride," "citizenship," and "gratitude."

Next, ADs were largely externally motivated to engage with PCA, namely for "professional development" purposes. The ADs discussed how there were high standards for professional development because they were athletics programs within educational settings. For example, Jordan said, "They were hammering down on the coach education piece at the MIAA [Massachusetts Interscholastic Athletic Association]. So when I received the call I thought this is a great opportunity for professional development." Similarly, Avery said, "It sounded like it could be a supplemental program to help me give my coaches professional development." Alex agreed, "It looked good for your program to be a part of it, to be affiliated with successful schools, to align ourselves with quality programs." In short, the primary motivation to partner with PCA was to

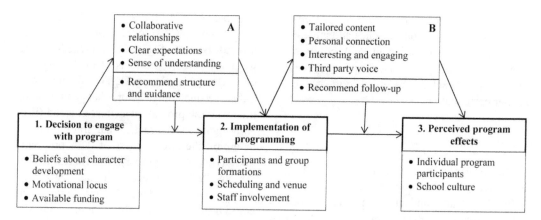

Note: The model depicts the process of engaging with the character education program from making the decision to engage to implementing the program to perceived program effects. The factors noted in Boxes "A" and "B" are intended to represent potential conceptual mediators and moderators.

FIGURE 1
. A Data-Derived Model for the Implementation of a Character Education Program
Through High School Athletics Programs

fulfill a professional development require-ment, but also because it "looked good" to uti-lize character education.

Finally, ADs did not have funds available to purchase a character education curriculum. Avery said, "I wouldn't take away anything right now that I currently do to bring this in. We're shoestring enough and we just need basic essentials (e.g., equipment, transporta-tion to/from competitions)." Alex said he would if he "could get funding to do it." Thus, ADs at public schools must also conduct a cost-benefit analysis when making decisions about the feasibility of engaging with character education programs through interscholastic sport.

Implementation

As shown in Figure 1, the ADs discussed their experiences implementing PCA program-ming. We have organized this section to first discuss logistical considerations for imple-menting PCA programming and then we high-light factors that may matter to facilitate

successful implementation. Finally, we present ADs' recommendations for implementation.

Logistics of Implementation. The ADs discussed three factors related to implementing the PCA program (Box 2 in Figure 1), includ-ing staff involvement, scheduling issues, and identifying target participants. First, the ADs noted that they had little or no administrative support suggesting "I didn't really have any help," or "I did it myself." Devon said, "I used my secretary to be present in some of the ses-sions. As far as communicating, I would just send the email to whatever team it might be to attend their session." Although one AD had some administrative support, the ADs agreed that implementing a curriculum through athlet-ics was particularly difficult because they did not have enough personnel support, and there were many "layers of control" that need to be penetrated to reach athletes directly (e.g., coaches).

Second, high school athletics function on a strict calendar set by the state athletics associ-ation which stipulates when teams can be selected, when first practices can occur, and when games will occur throughout the season.

Thus, adding a curriculum to the already complex calendar of high school athletics was "problematic schedulewise" or "a great idea on paper that was more difficult to execute." All ADs agreed that scheduling the PCA workshops needed to be more flexible and more amendable to high school athletics calendars.

Third, the ADs discussed how PCA's design allowed them to choose which individuals and groupings would receive the curriculum. Overall, the ADs agreed that the curriculum content was more suitable for younger athletes. For instance, ADs said PCA programming was "really geared for youth" or "geared a little too much toward youth sport." Avery suggested "if we can start at the youth level, they'll be familiar with it when they get to the high school program." Then, when athletes get to high school, Alex said, "Why not do it with the freshmen? What happens is the freshmen see how the JV [junior varsity] act and react. Then they move to JV and they watch the varsity."

A developmental progression may be necessary for athletes, but ADs agreed that the curriculum was most important for coaches and administrators. Alex said:

> The system comes from the leadership of an AD to show its coaches, student athletes, families, and school community we want to have things done in a positive manner. If our coaches listen and implement it, then I think we have a much better success rate in teaching our student athletes.

Indeed, ADs agreed that coaches were essential targets for character education. Jordan said, "I think where PCA would find the most influence is if they really dug their heels in with the coaching staff." Similarly, Alex said "I look at [character] more so with my coaching staff than I do the kids because I expect a lot more out of the coaches than I do out of the kids because they are adults." Together, these findings suggest that flexibility in implementation is necessary to deliver PCA programming effectively with high school athletes, coaches, and administrators.

Factors to Optimize Implementation. The ADs discussed three factors that would assist them in implementing PCA programming effectively and efficiently in their athletics programs, namely their expectations for PCA, their partnership with PCA, and feeling understood by PCA (Box A in Figure 1). First, the ADs did not have clear expectations about the curriculum. The ADs suggested that "nobody knew what to expect" or "had a ton of expectations going into it." Avery said, "For us, it was trying to delineate or affiliate what PCA was really trying to get accomplished. Okay, we're doing these workshops, but what does this really mean?" Similarly, Jordan said, "I'm not really sure what their overarching goal was." For some ADs, they did not understand what it would look like to implement the program in their school. Avery said, "I had no knowledge of PCA at all and I didn't quite know, even after talking to them, what this was gonna look like. I still don't know." The ADs thought that one way to clarify the expectations and to ease the transition into a partnership with PCA would be to have a local athletics director, who was both familiar with the PCA program and the responsibilities of an AD, serve as a mentor or local sponsor for the school.

Next, how the AD viewed his/her relationship with PCA mattered for implementation. The ADs viewed PCA as a "resource or facilitation," rather than a collaboration or partnership. The ADs felt as though PCA was not invested in the school and was "more of a guest." Avery wanted PCA to be more present in the partnership saying, "I just felt like we were kind of in a pocket over here, let's see what we can do with this group and then that's it." ADs did not view the relationship as collaborative, but viewed PCA as a resource to call upon when needed. When juxtaposed with the ADs' expectations, it is possible that viewing PCA as a resource could have led to their lack of use of programming.

Finally, the ADs thought PCA needed a better understanding of the high school context and how it differs from recreational youth sport. Jordan said, "It's not like an AAU [Amateur Athletic Union] program, it's not like a travel program, it's not like a club program. It's high school athletics, educational athletics." Alex discussed the hectic lives of high school athletes saying, "These kids nowadays are going out working five hour shifts after they go to practice until 10 o'clock at night. Then they're up until 2 in the morning doing homework. Their schedules are really busy." Jordan agreed that, "Besides coaching, whether they're a teacher or working insurance, they have a lot of demands. They may only have a short window of time. Leading into a season, every minute counts in trying to be with their team." The ADs thought PCA staff should have a clear understanding of high school athletics and be considerate of the context when planning program implementation.

Recommendations. To ease implementation, the ADs thought it would be helpful to have a "menu of options" from PCA to know the possibilities for the curriculum. Alex also thought more guidance with planning was needed:

> It may be best if PCA put out a syllabus that said "you're gonna have your workshop on this day ... then you should do a talking point ... then you should follow it up with this." It just gives you a schedule to look at and you can cater it to your own specific needs.

Thus, along with a clearer description of the possible options for PCA programming, the ADs thought it would be helpful to have a "syllabus" to help guide them through program implementation.

Program Effectiveness

The ADs discussed several factors related to program effectiveness. First, the ADs discussed any perceived effects they saw from participating in PCA programming. Next, there were several factors identified that may inhibit or promote program effectiveness.

Finally, the ADs offered recommendations related to enhancing program effectiveness.

Program Effects. The ADs discussed two areas of program effects, namely effects related to participants directly receiving the program and to the culture of the school (Box 3 in Figure 1). First, the ADs thought PCA programming was mostly effective to reinforce existing beliefs. Devon said, "I think it was helpful in a sense that it gave coaches a reassurance that they were doing some correct things." Moreover, PCA programming provided a shared language to speak about character. Coaches and athletes were able to "associate character with acronyms and terms." Perceived behavior change was larger among coaches than athletes. For example, Alex noted an increase in "the collegiality of the coaches," suggesting that, "I mean there's discussion that never took place. It's not only male to male coaches, it's male to female coaches." The ADs did not see large changes among athletes, but thought that it "instilled in them to be confident about what's going on, speak up when there might be an issue, and take care of one another. The emotional support the peers were providing for peers was actually pretty cool." In sum, the ADs believed that PCA programming was largely effective in reinforcing existing beliefs about character and providing terminology to discuss character in sport.

Although the ADs noted some small individual effects, they did not see a change to the culture of their schools or athletics programs. ADs had unique goals to create specific cultures for their schools and did not want to bring in PCA to create a new culture. Rather, ADs preferred to integrate the "PCA Way" into their own school cultures. For example, Jordan thought "There were definitely some things that could be pulled, but I wouldn't say our identity was a PCA school. I wouldn't really say that that's where we were at." Devon agreed saying, "I really didn't create an overall culture to say okay this is the philosophy we're gonna be following." Although these ADs thought that PCA could contribute positively to their school cultures, they did not think that PCA defined their school cultures.

Factors to Optimize Program Effects. There were multiple factors that mattered for program effectiveness, including tailored content, personal connections, interesting and engaging format, and third party voice (Box B in Figure 1). First, ADs thought that tailored content would be more effective for their athletes than universal content. ADs disliked a "one-size-fits-all" approach. Many of the ADs had particular areas (e.g., social media, hazing) they wanted to target with PCA programming because "every year you have a different group of kids with different challenges." Devon thought PCA needed "a little bit more prior knowledge about what the school needs." There were instances in which the ADs communicated with PCA about their particular programming needs, such as Devon who said, "I gave three bullet points of things that I was interested in and they covered it. It was awesome." The ADs wanted to tailor the program to their schools, but also to specific teams. For example, Alex said, "I would break it down team by team. When you have those discussions, kids can be frank with each other because they're gonna be side by side on the field or on the court." ADs' perspectives suggest that universal programming may not be as effective for their schools as tailored programming.

Next, the ADs thought it was important for PCA to make personal connections with the athletes in their schools. For example, Avery said, "They got a lot of powerful people on their boards, but how do we connect to that?" He went on to say, "I think they have national outreach, but if they could find a way to make it more local so that we all can get our connection, it would be better." Alex agreed that "there's gotta be some thought process as to how we can intertwine who the spokespeople are for PCA and the message that they're trying to get out to the high schools." Making this intentional connection with high school athletes was exemplified by Avery when he said: "We had a female [from PCA] who's African

American, who was an athlete. Our girls saw her and heard her story, which was more powerful than anything I could have ever put together." The ADs underscored the importance of connecting with high school athletes.

Third, PCA's message needed to be delivered in an interesting, engaging, and interactive format. ADs thought the workshops were "repetitive" and "too long to keep the athletes' attention." For example, Alex said, "To be honest, I was pretty burnt out on this. I didn't really feel like the workshops were changing our kids or coaches a whole lot. It came across as very repetitive at times." Jordan agreed saying "If it's hearing the same exact message multiple times, it almost becomes counterproductive at some point. It feels more like a waste of time." ADs thought that more discussion in the athlete workshops would be beneficial, such as Alex who said, "The kids are more talked to in the workshops, whereas the coaches are more discussion oriented. I think the kids need discussion." The workshops also needed to be short, which was stated succinctly by Avery who said, "I asked him not to be too long winded because they're gonna tune out after a while. So I asked him to hit on each point real quickly. And he did that. It worked." Thus, discussion-oriented workshops which are less repetitive and shorter may contribute to a more interesting, engaging, and interactive workshop format.

Finally, ADs thought one of the most valuable parts of PCA was having a third party voice convey the message. Devon said, "it's a different voice than my own. I've been saying [character is important] for the last 3 years, but it's better than hearing me speak over and over again." Alex agreed saying, "there's times when you bring someone else in to reinforce that fact that it's a different face, it's a different view, it's a different voice. I think it's that addition to the curriculum that worked." Having a third party deliver a message about character development helped reinforce the messages the ADs were already sending.

Recommendations. To optimize the potential for program effects, ADs wanted more follow-up from PCA, particularly with the coaches. ADs thought PCA was not engaged with the school deeply enough and, as Jordan said, there was "definitely a lack of support or follow up with the coaches about these kids." Avery described how the lack of follow up from PCA "left them hanging:"

> The other thing was the follow up for the coaches. After it was over, some of my coaches questioned what they got. We had the meeting in the beginning, but thought there would be some follow up with the coaches at the end of the season and that wasn't there.

Continued follow-up from PCA would help the ADs assess how well the program worked and make decisions about moving forward with the program.

DISCUSSION

Sport is a setting known to promote positive youth development (Holt, 2016). However, findings about whether sport promotes character are mixed (Bredemeier & Shields, 2006; Rudd, 2005), likely due to the wide variation in the quality of sport programs. Thus, character education may be necessary to ensure high quality sport environments that promote character attributes. Although there is much knowledge of effective character education in schools (Berkowitz et al., 2017), little is known about character education in interscholastic sport settings. The purpose of this study was to examine ADs' perspectives of PCA's programming and to generate hypotheses (Cattell, 1966) about the process involved in sport-based character education. Our hope is that this hypothesis-generation process can lead to ideas that will be tested in various, specific ways in different sport-based character education programs.

Character Education: Considerations for Interscholastic Sport

This study was grounded in the current state of character education in schools, in particular,

the PRIMED model of prioritizing character education, building positive Relationships, fostering Intrinsic motivation, being positive role Models, Empowering all stakeholders, and providing developmentally appropriate pedagogy (Berkowitz et al., 2017). We discuss our findings in the context of the PRIMED model in order to extend what is known about character education in schools to character education in interscholastic sport settings.

Prioritizing Character Education. For character education to be effective, character must be authentically prioritized (Berkowitz et al., 2017). The ADs in this study believed character was important, but did not seem to prioritize character in their athletics programs. Practically, the lack of character prioritization may have been because ADs did not have a clear understanding of PCA programming and were not trained well enough to maintain the programming after PCA personnel left the school. Thus, a primary focus among ADs might be *how* to prioritize character rather than *whether* to prioritize character. Prioritizing character in sport may involve reconceptualizing the definition of competition. Competition may be viewed through a metaphor of war (e.g., a battle to be won) or through a metaphor of partnership (e.g., an interdependent activity to support shared goals; Shields & Bredemeier, 2011; Shields, Funk, & Bredemeier, 2016a). We hypothesize that reconceptualizing the definition of competition to focus on partnership will lead to greater prioritization of character in sport.

There is evidence that athletes' orientation to competition matters for character attributes, such that partnership orientations predicted increased sportspersonship (Shields, Funk, & Bredemeier, 2016b), decreased moral disengagement (Shields, Funk, & Bredemeier, 2015), as well as increased grit (Shields, Funk & Bredemeier, 2018). Developing a partnership orientation to competition involves appreciating the role of the opponent, which PCA approaches by using the Latin root of the word competition, that is "to strive with," as opposed to the common understanding of competition meaning "to strive against" (Thompson, 2010). However, athletes need to learn the partnership concept and, as well, practice the partnership approach in context. As the concept of orientations to competition is relatively new to the literature (e.g., Shields & Bredemeier, 2011), learning how to develop partnership orientations may be a promising line for future research.

Building Positive Relationships. Effective character education involves building and nurturing positive relationships (Berkowitz et al., 2017). PCA's model of character education is largely focused on developing positive relationships between coaches and athletes. However, findings from this study suggest that the relationship between PCA and their partner organization (i.e., ADs in the current study) is also essential to authentically engage with PCA programming. Our findings suggest that ADs did not view their relationships with PCA as a partnership or collaboration, but rather as a resource. Moreover, ADs did not have clear expectations of the partnership from the outset and wanted more follow-up and presence from PCA in their schools. We hypothesize that collaboration, clear expectations, and follow-through will predict strong and positive relationships among the organizations offering character education and the administrators involved in implementing the curriculum in their schools.

An approach to relationship-building in sport was presented by Blom and colleagues (2015) in the RESPOND model. RESPOND involves codeveloping relevant, empowering, sustainable partnerships that promote local opportunities, networks, and development (Blom et al., 2015). Our findings suggest that sport-based character education should be relevant to athletes and coaches, be empowering for the coaches and athletes to engage with the curriculum, be sustainable through follow-up visits and continued consultation, and provide additional opportunities for growth in the school and athletics program. Specific strategies to enhance partnerships include (1) emphasizing shared leadership with regard

to content, context, expertise, and resources; (2) encouraging reciprocity, validation and trust; and (3) establishing clear expectations and roles at the outset (Blom et al., 2015). Future research should test how and which relationships foster successful integration of character education in sport.

Fostering Intrinsic Motivation. Character education should use strategies that promote internalization of specific character attributes the initiative targets (Berkowitz et al., 2017). In this study, ADs' intrinsic motivation to engage with PCA was lacking and there were no clear strategies for improvement. That is, ADs engaged with PCA largely for free professional development and a positive image. Moreover, ADs' demanding responsibilities and limited resources constrained their time and ability to authentically devote their athletics programs to character education. We hypothesize that intrinsic motivation to engage with character education is especially important when the external constraints on administrators to implement the curriculum are high. Explicit strategies are needed to foster intrinsic motivation among ADs.

A strong predictor of intrinsic motivation is an individual's goal orientation, such that a mastery orientation (e.g., focus on personal improvement) is associated with higher intrinsic motivation than a performance orientation (e.g., focus on winning or looking good; e.g., Ferrer-Caja & Weiss, 2000). Thus, a promising approach to increase ADs' intrinsic motivation and subsequently, coaches' and athletes' intrinsic motivation, may be to shift the focus away from the positive image a character education curriculum provides for a school and toward the positive effects individuals experience from character education. However, more research is needed on the positive effects of character education in sport. Moreover, as sport is a dual-goal setting focused on winning and life skills (e.g., Gould & Carson, 2008), future research should also disentangle the relation between the development of character attributes and performance outcomes (e.g., winning records).

Positive Role Models. Adults should model their expectations of youth for character education to be effective (Berkowitz et al., 2017). The ADs in this study suggested that coaches are the most important role models for athletes and, thus, should be a primary focus of PCA. Indeed, just as teachers are important for character development in schools (Berkowitz et al., 2017), coaches are highly influential role models for youth athletes' character (Ferris, Ettekal, Agans, & Burkhard, 2015). A challenge may be that coaching behaviors are difficult to change, perhaps because of the prevalent focus on winning in sport. For example, positive coaching behaviors diminished among coaches who were evaluated based on their athletes' scoreboard performance (Iachini, 2013). Thus, athletics administrators will also have to shift their standards away from strictly performance outcomes in order to promote positive role modeling among coaches. Nevertheless, coaches should resist the pressure of using ineffective practices, such as focusing on winning and scoreboard results, and prioritize character in their coach practices. We hypothesize that defining success in athletics programs based on character outcomes, as well as winning, will lead to more positive role modeling in interscholastic sport.

A strategy for positive role modeling may be found in the power of a common language. For example, ADs in this study thought PCA's terminology was "sticky" and useful for coaches and athletes to identify and practice different character attributes. However, this finding was also coupled with some ADs' perceptions that the programming and some of its terminology was more geared toward younger athletes. Thus, a shared language can provide a way of promoting positive role modeling, but coaches and athletes should be empowered to develop their own language that is most relevant to their teams and athletes. A shared language that is developed, celebrated, and practiced by coaches and athletes may promote positive role modeling within the sport environment, as well as carry over to other settings, such as athletes' classrooms.

Empowering Stakeholders. Effective character education programs share power with stakeholders (Berkowitz et al., 2017). In this study, ADs did not perceive stakeholders, such as themselves, coaches, or athletes as having a voice in the programming. ADs largely experienced a universal program implemented in a "one-size-fits-all" format. Previous research suggests that youth programming that is tailored to an individual's or group's specific needs is more effective in promoting empowerment than universal programming (Simpkins & Riggs, 2014). ADs in this study suggested that PCA made few personal connections with their athletes, but when personal connections were made, they were very powerful. Therefore, we may hypothesize that involving stakeholders in determining what type of programming is needed, how to deliver the program, and to whom to deliver the program will lead to more effective character education in sport.

Culturally responsive organized activity systems provide an excellent framework to provide programming which empowers the stakeholders and gives the individuals involved in the program a voice (Simpkins, Riggs, Okamoto, Ettekal, & Ngo, 2016). Our findings suggest that ADs did not want to impose a new PCA culture on their school, but rather wanted to integrate PCA into their own cultures. Integrating an existing curriculum into a school's culture involves listening to the specific youth about their needs and preferences, and using methods of delivery that are important and useful to those specific youth. Stakeholders (e.g., community members, teachers, coaches, parents, and youth) have important knowledge about the specific character needs, of the specific youth athletes served, in the specific types of sport, and in specific historical times. We hypothesize that tailoring character education to this "specificity" in sport (cf. Bornstein, 2017) will promote stakeholder empowerment.

Developmentally Appropriate Programming. Pedagogy should be developmentally appropriate in effective character education (Berkowitz & Bier, 2014: Berkowitz et al., 2017). Many of the ADs in the current study thought PCA's programming and terminology was geared toward younger youth. Moreover, the ADs thought PCA workshops needed to be more interesting, engaging, and interactive for high school athletes. As the ADs noted, one size does not fit all and they preferred programming that matched the developmental phase of their high school athletes. A primary psychological need of adolescence is to feel a sense of belonging and mattering (Deci & Ryan, 2011). One way to promote athletes' belonging and mattering is to give them a voice in the programming they experience. In this study, athletes had little or no voice in the curriculum content they experienced (e.g., what character attributes they focused on), where the curriculum was delivered (e.g., in a classroom versus on the field), or how the content was delivered (e.g., lecture versus discussion-based approaches). The ADs felt that PCA did not fully understand their high schools or the demands of high school athletes. We hypothesize that top-down approaches to character education, such as by implementing programming in which only adults have voice, will lead to decreased effectiveness.

The ADs also wanted programming to be provided in a developmental progression (e.g., new compared to returning athletes). Developmental needs should be considered, but also the specific needs of an athlete along a specific trajectory in their sport involvement. There are multiple pathways of sport involvement marked by if and when an athlete specializes in sport (Côté, Baker, & Abernathy, 2007). According to the developmental model of sport participation, sampling multiple sports early and continuing recreational play promotes increased performance, enjoyment, and personal development, whereas early specialization promotes increased performance, but at the cost of athlete enjoyment and burnout (Côté, et al., 2007). We suggest that successful character education programming may necessarily depend on the developmental phase of sport engagement. For example, specialized athletes and highly competitive coaches may be more resistant to changing their orientation to competition than recreational athletes and coaches. A clear hypothesis, then, is that character education in sport should align with youth developmental phase, as well as their pathway of sport involvement.

CONCLUSIONS

Derived from knowledge about effective character education in schools (e.g., Berkowitz & Bier, 2014), the current study sought to examine ADs' perspectives of PCA's sport-based character education program and to generate hypotheses (Cattell, 1966) about the process involved in sport-based character education. As we have noted, future tests of the hypotheses we have generated will require testing through use of specific operationalizations and associated measures linked to the general constructs identified in the hypotheses. Nevertheless, a contribution of the present study is to point future researchers to several key constructs and hypothesized associations between constructs that require further refinement in diverse sport-based character education programs. Importantly, such future tests should also involve tests of causality. The data involved in the current article reflected retrospective accounts of ADs' engagement with a character education curriculum in their high school athletics programs. Thus, we did not test causal effects of character education in sport on athletes' character. Next steps involve integrating the hypotheses generated in the present research into a model of the process of engaging with sport-based character education. Evidence derived from such theory-guided research may promote successful implementation and effective character education in sport.

Character development through sport is not certain and may require intentional efforts to shift away from a focus on performance goals (e.g., winning) and, thus, to prioritize character (Bredemeier & Shields, 2006). The hypotheses generated from the ADs' views point to several facets of a process that may need to be instantiated for character education in sport to be effective. Key findings include the need for positive and collaborative relationships between athletics administrators and organizations offering sport-based character education, tailored programming that incorporates stakeholders' (e.g., coaches, parents, athletes) input, and positive change and modeling of character at the "top" (i.e., administration) in order to promote change on the "bottom" (i.e., coaches and athletes). Moreover, reconceptualizing athletics administrators', coaches', and athletes' orientations to competition was a common theme, such that a partnership orientation to sport may help promote engagement with character education and increase its effectiveness. Learning more about the view of ADs, and other key informants, is important to create effective character education programs in sport settings. Future research should test the hypotheses presented in the current study and, as well, pursue additional questions concerning the effectiveness of sport-based character education.

REFERENCES

Berkowitz, M. W., & Bier, M. C. (2014). Research-based fundamentals of the effective promotion of character development in schools. In L. Nucci, D. Narvaez, & T. Krettenauer (Eds.), *Handbook on moral and character education* (pp. 248–260). New York, NY: Routledge.

Berkowitz, M. W., Bier, M. C. & McCauley, B. (2017). Effective features and practices that support character development. *Journal of Character Education, 13*(1), 33–51.

Blom, L. C., Judge, L., Whitley, M. A., Gerstein, L., Huffman, A., & Hillyer, S. (2015). Sport for development and peace: Experiences conducting U.S. and international programs. *Journal of Sport Psychology in Action, 6,* 1–16.

Bornstein, M. H. (2017). The specificity principle in acculturation science. *Perspectives on Psychological Science, 12,* 3–45.

Bredemeier, B., & Shields, D. (1986). Game reasoning and interactional morality. *Journal of Genetic Psychology, 147,* 257–275.

Bredemeier, B., & Shields, D. (2006). Sports and character development. *President's Council on Physical Fitness and Sports Research Digest, 7,* 1–8.

Cattell, R. B. (Ed.). (1966). Psychological theory and scientific method. In *Handbook of multivariate experimental psychology* (pp. 1–18). Chicago, IL: Rand McNally.

Côté, J., Baker, J., & Abernathy, B. (2007). Practice and play in the development of sport expertise. In R. Eklund & G. Tenebaum (Eds.), *Handbook of sport psychology* (pp. 184–202). Hoboken, NJ: Wiley.

Deci, E. L., & Ryan, R. M. (2011). Levels of analysis, regnant causes of behavior, and well-being: The role of psychological needs. *Psychological Inquiry, 22,* 17–22.

Doty, J. P., & Lumpkin, A. (2010). Do sports build or reveal character? An exploratory study at one service academy. *Physical Educator, 67,* 18–24.

Duda, J. L., & Nicholls, J.G. (1992). Dimensions of achievement motivation in schoolwork and sport. *Journal of Educational Psychology, 84,* 290–299.

Eccles, J. S., & Gootman, J. A. (Eds.). (2002). *Community programs to promote youth development.* Washington, DC: National Academy Press.

Emerson, R. M., Fretz, R. I., & Shaw, L. L. (1995). *Writing ethnographic fieldnotes.* Chicago, IL: University of Chicago Press.

Ettekal, A. V., Konowitz, L., Agans, J. P., Syer, T., & Lerner, R. M. (2017). Researcher-practitioner collaborations: Applying developmental science to understand sport participation and positive youth development. *Journal of Community Engagement and Higher Education, 9,* 29–45.

Ferrer-Caja, E., & Weiss, M. R. (2000). Predictors of intrinsic motivation among adolescent students in physical education. *Research Quarterly for Exercise & Sport, 71,* 267–279.

Ferris, K. A., Ettekal, A. V., Agans, J. P., & Burkhard, B. M. (2015). Character development through youth sport: High school coaches' perspectives about a character-based education program. *Journal of Youth Development, 10*(3), 127–140.

Gould, D., & Carson, S. (2008). Life skills development through sport: Current status and future directions. *International Review of Sport and Exercise Psychology, 1,* 58–78.

Holt, N. L. (2016). *Positive youth development through sport* (2nd ed.). New York, NY: Routledge.

Hsieh, H., & Shannon, S. E. (2005). Three approaches to qualitative content analysis. *Qualitative Health Research, 15,* 1277–1288.

Iachini, A. L. (2013). Development and empirical examination of a model of factors influencing coaches provision of autonomy-support. *International Journal of Sports Science & Coaching, 8,* 661–675.

Lerner, R. M., & Callina, K. S. (2014). The study of character development: Toward tests of a relational developmental systems model. *Human Development, 57,* 322–346.

Lerner, R. M., Lerner, J. V., Bowers, E., & Geldhof, G. J. (2015). Positive youth development and relational developmental systems. In W. F. Overton & P. C. Molenaar (Eds.), *Theory and method: Vol. 1. Handbook of child psychology and developmental science* (7th ed. pp. 607–651). Hoboken, NJ: Wiley.

Maholmes, V., & Lomonaco, C. G. (Eds.). (2010). *Applied research in child and adolescent development: A practical guide.* New York, NY: Taylor & Francis.

Miles, M. B., & Huberman, A. M. (1994). *Qualitative data analysis: An expanded sourcebook* (2nd ed.). Newbury Park, CA: SAGE.

Nucci, L. P. (2017). Character: A multi-faceted developmental system. *Journal of Character Education, 13*(1), 1–16.

Nucci, L. P. (2001). *Education in the moral domain.* Cambridge, England: Cambridge University Press.

Positive Coaching Alliance. (2017). Mission & History. Retrieved from http://positivecoach.org/mission-history/

Rudd, A. (2005). Which "character" should sport develop? *Physical Educator, 62,* 205–212.

Ryan, G. W., & Bernard, H. R. (2003). Techniques to identify themes. *Field Methods, 15,* 85–109.

Sabo, D., & Veliz, P. (2008). *Go out and play: Youth sports in America.* East Meadow, NY: Women's Sports Foundation.

Shields, D. L., & Bredemeier, B. L. (2011). Contest, competition, and metaphor. *Journal of Philosophy of Sport, 38,* 27–38.

Shields, D. L., Funk, C. D., & Bredemeier, B. L. (2015). Contesting orientations: Measure construction and the prediction of sportspersonship. *Psychology of Sport & Exercise, 20,* 1–10.

Shields, D. L., Funk, C. D., & Bredemeier, B. L. (2016a). The moral frameworks and foundations of contesting orientations. *Journal of Sport and Exercise Psychology, 38,* 117–127.

Shields, D. L., Funk, C. D., & Bredemeier, B. L. (2016b). Testing contesting theory: Conceptual metaphors and prosocial behavior. *Psychology of Sport and Exercise, 27,* 213–221.

Shields, D. L., Funk, C. D., & Bredemeier, B. L. (2018). Can contesting orientations predict grittier, more self-controlled athletes? *The Journal of Positive Psychology, 13*(5), 440–448.

Simpkins, S. D., & Riggs, N. R. (2014). Cultural competence in afterschool programs. *New directions for youth development, 144,* 105–117.

Simpkins, S. D., Riggs, N., Okamoto, D., Ettekal, A. V., & Ngo, B. (2016). Designing culturally responsive organized after-school activities. *Journal of Adolescent Research, 31,* 11–36.

Thomas, D. R. (2006). A general inductive approach for analyzing qualitative evaluation data. *American Journal of Evaluation, 27,* 237–246.

Thompson, J. (2010). *Developing winners in sports and life: The power of double-goal coaching.* Portola Valley, CA: Balance Sports.

Vandell, D. L., Larson, R. W., Mahoney, J. L., & Watts, T. W. (2015). Children's organized activities. In R. M. Lerner (Ed.), *Handbook of child psychology and developmental science* (7th ed., pp. 1–40). Hoboken, NJ: Wiley.

Yohalem, N., Wilson-Ahlstrom, A., Fischer, S., & Shinn, M. (2007). *Measuring youth program quality: A guide to assessment tools.* Washington, DC: The Forum for Youth Investment.

A NEW PERSPECTIVE
Spontaneous Character Education Using Positive Causal Attribution Training

Sarah Hamsher
Indian Wesleyan University

Character education in schools is implemented using different approaches. The current practices related to character education, though, include educators implementing preplanned lessons and activities from published programs. Yet, these current practices have mixed reviews in large- and small-scale studies. The purpose of this article is to provide a new perspective and approach for character education; one that is based on spontaneity using positive causal attribution training (PCAT). Strategies for implementing spontaneous character education using PCAT are also provided.

VIGNETTE

A basketball coach had a time out with his team. He was visibly upset about the previous play and let his team know his frustration with firm corrective feedback. Most interestingly, though, he pulled one player aside before the time out ended and said, "Tyler, you were really persistent out there on defense. You didn't let your man get around you. Good job." The type of feedback the coach gave was impressive. The coach labeled his player with a positive causal attribute, was very specific about how his player displayed the attribute, and provided the feedback during a sponta-neous, unplanned moment. This is a shining example of how schools could provide character education in a spontaneous manner.

INTRODUCTION

Character education can be defined as "intentional implementations that organize behaviors according to main human values and are provided with the aim of training academically successful individuals" (Katmilis, Eksi, & Osturk, 2011, p. 855). This type of programming encourages students to act on values, such as, *respect, civic virtues and citizenship, responsibility for others, self-control, loyalty,*

• **Correspondence concerning this article should be addressed to:**   Sarah Hamsher, sarah.hamsher@indwes.edu

ISSN 1543-1223

courage, perseverance, and *honesty,* all of which encourages them to enact goodness (Davis, 2006; Huitt, 2004; Lickona, 1991; Niemic, Rashid, & Spinella, 2012; Shields 2011) that can positively impact either or both academic performance and moral character (Haynes & Thomas, 2011).

The terms *values* and *character* are closely related. *Values* involve orientations and guiding principles, such as self-control, responsibility, and perseverance (Huitt, 2004a; Ryan & Bohlin, 1999). *Character,* then, requires action on values, which manifests itself in observable behaviors (Huitt, 2004a). For example, an athlete demonstrates the value of respect when she shakes an opposing athlete's hand, which is "good" character. When values are active and applied, one's character is evident. Therefore, values are one of the foundations of character, and character education involves guidance on how to act on one's values.

Despite noble intentions and a variety of ways character education programs have been implemented, their effectiveness has been weak (Social and Character Development Research Consortium, 2010; U.S. Department of Education, 2007). Character education using positive causal attribution training (PCAT) in spontaneous moments, which is the focus of this paper, may provide an alternative to typical implementations.

Character education programs in schools across America are implemented using different approaches. For example, character education has been integrated into after school programs (Hill, Milliken, Goff, Clark, & Gagnon, 2015); sports (Power, 2014); discipline specific programming such as art (Hyungsook, 2014), social studies (Katilmis, Eksi, & Ozturk., 2011), cinema (Russell & Waters, 2014), and religious studies (Roso, 2013); and while building caring relationship between teachers and students (Sojourner, 2014). These approaches to character education are usually in the form of preplanned lessons or activities promoted by a particular published program. Empirical studies, however, do not yield data indicating effectiveness of these programs.

What Works Clearinghouse (WWC), an agency of the Institute of Education Sciences, collects evidence on the efficacy of a variety of curricula, including character education programs. The last comprehensive evaluation of such programs occurred in 2007 when WWC examined 93 studies involving 41 programs. WWC found only 13 character education programs that evidence "positive effects to no discernible effects" in the three areas: behavior; knowledge, attitudes & values; and academic achievement. Of these 13 programs, there is only one program in each category that has "strong evidence of a positive effect with no overriding contrary evidence" (U.S. Department of Education, 2007, p. 2).

Then in 2010, the U.S. Department of Education (USDOE) and the National Center for Education Research (NCER) found dismal results in their comprehensive study that measured the wide-spread effectiveness of seven character education programs thought to be the most popular in the United States. This study titled, "Efficacy of Schoolwide Programs to Promote Social and Character Development and Reduce Problem Behavior in Elementary School Children" involved following 6,000 students from third through fifth grades and measured 20 possible behavioral and academic outcomes. While the results of the study showed an increase in character-based activities in the classroom and schools receiving social and character development curricula (SACD), it most importantly reported that "there were no differences in students' social and emotional competence, behaviors, academic performance, or perceptions of school climate between students in schools implementing one of the seven SACD programs and those in the control schools" (Social and Character Development Research Consortium, 2010, par. 5). There have been no such studies evaluating the efficacy of character education sponsored by the federal government since 2010.

Conversely, four studies emphasize the positive impact of character education programs on academic performance in schools.

Berkowitz and Bier (2005) identified 54 out of 100 character education programs as reputable, 33 of which had scientific evidence supporting their effectiveness. In addition, Benninga, Berkowitz, Kuehn, and Smith (2006) found that character education positively affected academic performance in 120 elementary schools. Finally, Marshall, Caldwell, and Foster (2011) found in two, multi-year studies that character education programs improved overall school climate and academic performance. While the findings in these studies are promising for character education programming, the small number of programs found effective do not indicate national, wide-spread positive outcomes.

Several scholars have provided explanations regarding the mixed results of character education along with possible alternatives. First, teacher preparation programs lack training in character education (DeRoche & Williams, 1998; Milson, 1999; Ryan, 1997). Ryan (1997) specifically suggests these programs instead should train preservice teachers to be persons of good character and morality; see the development of students' moral life and character as professional responsibility; engage students in moral discourse; articulate their own moral principles without seeking to conform students; help students empathize with the concerns of others; establish a positive moral classroom climate; and engage students in activities in school and in the community to develop ethics and altruism (pp. 88–89). As a result, teachers would be better prepared to teach character education programs upon entry into their first teaching position.

Ryan (2013) also contends that human behavior cannot be measured. Behavior is not a tangible skill that can be observed like those associated with reading and math. Due to the abstract nature of one's character, this scholar suggests the states should not be responsible for deciding what "character" means and impose their own positions. Instead, character education is successful when it connects to students' "deepest goals and purposes, when it is directed toward the acquisition of virtues, and

when it has the support and cooperation of those most responsible for their well-being, their parents" (p. 145). Thus, Ryan believes character education should be deeply personal and provided by individuals who know the student the best.

Finally, Chen (2013) suggests character education in the United States lacks uniformity, creating a variety of interpretations and consequent confusion. This scholar alternatively suggests moral virtues provided in character education programs should be individualized according to one's temperament. Individualizing character programs means creating relevant situations to assist students in confronting the adverse affects of their temperament with virtuous outcomes. This alternative would create uniformity in character education programs and minimize the variety of their interpretations.

These scholars who have described possible reasons for the mixed results in character education programming and potential alternatives promote one main theme: character education programs need to be personal to students. If current approaches to character education are not personal to students and they do not yield evidence of wide-spread positive outcomes, other approaches need to be considered. One approach to character education that has the potential to be personal and relevant to students uses positive causal attribution training (PCAT), which includes drawing attention to positive causal attributions, or what many schools label as "good" character. The framework of this type of character education integrates an additional component missing in the various character education programs described in this article: spontaneity.

The spontaneity aspect of PCAT is integrated much like the spontaneity provided by the basketball coach in the vignette. Educators verbally describe their interpretations of students' positive attributes associated with behaviors they witness in unplanned settings. It intertwines even the smallest occurrences in a school day with character education. The consequence is students become more aware of the connection between their positive causal attributes and the moment-by-moment tasks and decisions in which they engage, potentially training them to think differently about themselves. The end goal of this approach to character education is students' improved self-efficacy. Therefore, the purpose of this article is to describe positive causal attribution training (PCAT) as the crux for spontaneous character education and provide strategies for its implementation.

CLARIFICATION OF TERMS

In order to clarify the direction of this article, two terms need defined. The terms *attributes* and *causal attribution training* are interrelated yet they are distinct. *Attributes* are beliefs about causality, positive or negative (Weiner, 1986); they include reasons "why" one behaved in a certain manner. The reasons or beliefs are related to one's deeply rooted values, such as respect. *Causal attribution training* involves a process of identifying a person's beliefs about the causes of his or her own failures and successes to promote future motivation for achievement (Roberston, 2000). For example, an athlete may need causal attribution training to help identify her attribute of respect for others as a possible reason she shook an opposing athlete's hand. Thus, attributes include values. Causal attribution training, then, can guide students' thinking in order to identify the specific values causing behavior-related decisions.

KEY THEORETICAL FRAMEWORKS

This new perspective on spontaneous character education using PCAT is grounded in three theories.

Self-Efficacy Theory

First, Albert Bandura's self-efficacy theory (1977) posits that an individual's belief in his

or her capacity to execute behaviors influences the ability to produce specific performance attainments. More specifically, Bandura (1995) defines perceived self-efficacy as, "beliefs in one's capabilities to organize and perform the courses of action required to manage prospective situations. Efficacy beliefs influence how people think, feel, motivate themselves, and act" (p. 2). Thus, individuals who can influence controllable circumstances can conceptualize desirable outcomes and inhibit undesired ones. Personal control of beliefs about capabilities that cause behaviors are central to self-efficacy. Furthermore, these beliefs that cause behaviors can be developed in four ways: mastery experiences, vicarious experiences, social persuasion, and enhancing physical status. Bandura's theory has been confirmed as studies show attribution training has been a successful intervention used to address learners' self-efficacy (Margolis & McCabe, 2004; Scott, 1996) and self-concept (Kozminsky & Kozminsky, 2003; Robertson, 2000).

Two aspects related to the social persuasion method of developing self-efficacy are of particular interest to this article. First, one's beliefs about perceived self-efficacy can be altered through social persuasion. This method indicates "To the extent that persuasive boosts in perceived self-efficacy lead people to try hard enough to succeed, self-affirming beliefs promote development of skills and a sense of personal efficacy" (p. 4). This facet of self-efficacy theory suggests that the personal beliefs one has about his or her capacity to execute behaviors are malleable. This conclusion is supported by Graham and Weiner (1996), who indicate personal beliefs about the efficacy to perform well on a task are founded on unstable, causal attributions. The instability of causal attributions is one of the foundational precepts of spontaneous character education using PCAT. This approach to character education includes positively influencing self-efficacy related to demonstrating good character. For example, students' self-efficacy can be influenced by external variables (i.e., positive teacher feedback) that speak to internal, unstable variables (one's values evidenced in observed character). As PCAT is translated into the school setting, this training could be a catalyst for improving students' self-efficacy and self-concept, both of which may impact achievement.

The second aspect of social persuasion of interest to this article is the inherent need for social interactions (also see Bandura's social learning theory). The need for social interaction speaks directly to the nature of character education through PCAT, which requires educators to relate to students personally and spontaneously. Educators are ripe for this influential role as research indicates their influence can have positive effects on classroom behaviors (Griggs, Gagnon, Huelsman, Kidder-Ashley, & Ballard, 2009), peer relationships (Howes, Hamilton & Metheson, 1994), disruptions in class (Marzano, Marzano, & Pickering, 2003) and overall commitment to learning (Doll, Spies, LeClari, Kurien, & Foley, 2010).

Attribution Theory

The second theory in the theoretical framework of this article is attribution theory, upon which Weiner (1985) expands upon Bandura's self-efficacy theory. Weiner posits causal attributions (a) are influenced by outcomes (e.g., passing or failing a test), and (b) have an effect on future behaviors because attributions influence students' choice, intensity, and persistence. There are three dimensions of causality: locus, stability, and controllability. Locus refers to the affect success or failure has on self-esteem and pride. Stability refers to an attribute that is not expected to change (e.g., aptitude). Controllability, then, is related to internally managed variables (e.g., effort) affecting successes or failures. As Chodkiewicz and Boyle (2014) simply state, this theory seeks to understand the thinking process that people use to explain why an event occurred (p. 78).

The attribution theory, according to Graham and Weiner (1996), is most often applied to academic settings. Yet, the premise of attribution theory has the potential to be generalized to spontaneous character education using PCAT. As previously supported by the self-efficacy theory, causal attributions are malleable because they are unstable. Attribution theory extends upon this premise by suggesting causal attributions are malleable because they are unstable *and* controllable. Thus, causal attributions have the potential to not only be influenced by educators but also managed by students. If causal attributions are unstable and controllable, one's attributional thinking (thought process related to deep-seeded beliefs that affect self-efficacy and observed character) can change from negative to positive. Spontaneous character education using PCAT, then, can be a method for influencing students' thinking in such a manner. This approach to character education requires educators to provide feedback to students about their deep-seeded beliefs (i.e., values) in action, which are controllable and unstable. Furthermore, if students then develop a healthy sense of self and feel ownership over positive attributions, their perceived self-efficacy and consequent levels of achievement can increase (Kozminsky & Kozminsky, 2003; Schunk & Ertmer, 1999).

Action Learning Theory

The third theoretical framework on which this article is based is action learning theory pioneered by Reg Revans. Action learning theory is a form of experiential learning, which proposes that learning by doing and frequent dialogue produce both personal and organizational learning (Dominguez & Hager, 2013, p. 176). As action learning theory relates to PCAT, Huitt (2004b) indicates that the act of valuing is a process of implementation as well as development. That is, it is important to move beyond thinking and feeling to acting. There needs to be specific opportunities for learners to act on their values.

In prior work, Huitt (2004a) suggests as students reflect on their behavior, it adds to the knowledge base, strengthens their thinking skills, and impacts their values. Huitt also purports it is critically important to help students make explicit one's own knowledge base, value system, and the process of committing and planning so as to make particular behaviors more intentional in the future. The precepts of action learning theory support the premise of PCAT, which is for students to learn about character by doing. If students become more aware of the values that cause certain behaviors by seeing them in action, they have the potential to strengthen their knowledge base about personal self-efficacy and be more intentional about enacting positive character.

This triad of theories provides the framework for spontaneous character education using PCAT. In this proposed method of implementing character education, all three theories are manifested. Namely, the educator socially interacts with a student immediately after an observed behavior in order to verbally identify the underlying value in which the behavior is rooted. In such an instance, the student also becomes aware that he or she has acted on an existing positive value. Ultimately, this social interaction is an effort by the educator to positively influence the student's attributional thinking and consequent self-efficacy.

EFFECTIVE PRAISE

Praise is a verbal statement that communicates positive feedback to a student (Simonsen, Myers, & DeLuca, 2010 p. 303). Brophy (1981), though, gives a much more precise definition as he indicates praise is "to commend the worth of or to express approval or admiration" (p. 5). Brophy continues to describe praise as statements that "express positive teacher affect (surprise, delight, excitement) and/or place the student's behavior in context by giving information about its value or its implications about the student's status" (p. 6).

Praise, according to Brophy, should only be used as a reinforcer if certain criteria are implemented. First, praise must be contingent. When provided, praise must be contingent on performance of the behavior to be reinforced (provided more infrequently than frequently). Second, praise must be specific, meaning praise should specify the particulars of the behavior being reinforced. This means praise must be specifically associated with the behavior that exemplifies the value. And, third, praise must be sincere. The praise must sound sincere and credible, as well as varied according to different situations and preferences of the student.

When considering the description of praise, it can be concluded that PCAT is a form of praise. PCAT requires praise related to unstable and controllable causal attributions. Brophy (1981) suggests that the attribution a teacher includes in praise statements impacts the level of influence the evaluative feedback has on students. For example, a teacher who praises students' achievement and tells them that they are "smart" may teach students to attribute their success to a stable and uncontrollable factor. But, teachers who praise students for working hard enough to achieve a goal will train the students to attribute their success to unstable effort factors (p. 23). It is during the latter context when praise is most effective, according this same scholar, and it is during this latter context that supports the guiding principles of PCAT.

Notably, Graham and Weiner (1996) emphasize the notion that individuals are biased in their ability to understand causal attributions. These experts use the metaphor that individuals are scientists who desire to understand the world but use "naive statistical techniques" to do so (p. 71). As a result, individuals have the potential to over- or underestimate causal attributions. This notion implies the need for guidance for students as they identify causal attributions. Therefore, in order for PCAT to be effective, educators need to include specific components in their feedback to students. The feedback needs to include (a) a praise word or phrase (e.g., *well done* or *excellent*); (b) a description of the specific, social or academic behavior exhibited by the student; and (c) the controllable, unstable, positive causal attribution. For example, a teacher might say, "Tony, excellent work on your science project. Despite wanting to focus on basketball, you made time for this project. You were self-disciplined." From such feedback, a student hears (a) the praise word *excellent*; (b) the specific behavior of prioritizing his science project; and (c) the controllable, unstable, positive causal attribution: *self-disciplined*. By hearing that he is *self-disciplined*, Tony has a chance to hear the possible attribution (i.e., root cause) why he made a good decision. Thus, Tony experienced spontaneous character education that may train him to think positively about his self-efficacy on a routine, school-based task.

MALADAPTIVE ATTRIBUTIONAL THINKING

While the goals of current character education programs is to help students "organize behaviors according to main human values" in order to become academically successful, not all students respond positively to such programs. In fact, many students have developed maladaptive (negative) attributional thinking, a way of thinking that can inhibit the goals of character education programs. The potential exists, though, to offset this type of thinking with intentional PCAT.

Maladaptive attributional thinking is characterized by the belief that failure is due to stable, internal causes such as low ability and success is a result of unstable, external causes such as luck (Robertson, 2000). For example, a student with maladaptive attributional thinking might say, "There is no way I could have passed that test. It was hard and I'm not that smart." According to Chodkiewicz and Boyle (2014), when students have maladaptive attributional thinking, they feel less motivated and confident than students with positive attributional thinking. These students engage less in positive learning behaviors, such as persisting on difficult questions, and engage more in behaviors that are destructive to their learning process, such as task avoidance. Students with maladaptive attributional thinking may conclude that their efforts are unrelated to achievement outcomes and, therefore, are futile (Fulk & Mastropieri, 1990; Pearl, 1982). These students may ask, "Why try when I'm just going to fail?" In turn, maladaptive attributional thinking negatively impacts future learning and academic performance. It is, therefore, the students' emotional and behavioral reactions to their perceptions about themselves that influence academic achievement (Chodkiewicz & Boyle, 2014). In order to train students to think differently about themselves, educators can provide moment-by-moment character education using PCAT on routine tasks, however short the task and even if the task appears to be a failure. Thus, educators need to look for the positive in the negative.

STRATEGIES FOR IMPLEMENTATION

Knowing character education is often thought of as a separate program in schools, likened to having its own silo, and it has weak empirical evidence for effectiveness, perhaps teachers need to place the protocol for implementing current character education programs aside in order to reimagine implementing the program with a spontaneous paradigm. This new perspective for implementation could train students to consciously associate their behaviors with specific, positive, causal attributes. This article so far has provided the theoretical framework with related literature for the foundation for spontaneous character education using PCAT. Therefore, described below are six strategies for implementing this approach to character education.

Learn It: Attribution Definitions

First, educators need to know what positive causal attributions, or what many schools label "good" character, look like in the everyday school context. Thus, educators need to take initiative to learn the definitions of and be able to distinguish among such character values as *effort, initiative, diligence, self-discipline, helpfulness, preparedness, commitment, perseverance, responsibility, trustworthiness*, and *compassion*. Educators can learn these attributions using resources such as Charactercounts.org that describes the "The Six Pillars of Character" or Charactered.net that describes eleven common, core values for character education programs.

Identify It: Scan Students

Second, educators need to not only learn the values but also identify them when they are demonstrated by students. It means learning to differentiate similar positive causal attributions that have similar constructs, such as *care* and *respect*, as they occur in observable behavior, which goes beyond just reading about them. This skill requires intentional practice while simply scanning students as they interact with each other and engage in the school context. For example, a teacher may witness a student in the hallway who picks up someone's dropped book, which is evidence of *helpfulness*. Or, an educator may notice a struggling student who works and works to solve a difficult problem, which is evidence of *perseverance*. The values of *helpfulness* and *perseverance* were acted upon by picking up the book and working hard on the difficult problem, respectively. By intentionally scanning students' behaviors as they occur, educators are more likely to see positive causal attributions as the root cause of the decisions students make and actions they take.

Provide it: Take the Time

Third, educators need to purposefully and intentionally take time to verbally describe to students the positive causal attributions associated with the specific behaviors students exhibit. It is easy for teachers, principals, aides, and administrative staff to focus on their "to-do" lists throughout the day and not praise students for their positive character. Yet, research indicates that praise, especially when it is behavior specific, provided with authenticity, and focuses on students' accomplishments, consistently results in improved student academic and social behaviors (Brophy, 1981; Cherne, 2009; Sugai, 2007). Academic literature also indicates teacher-student relationships that emphasize care and encouraging feedback positively impact students' emotional, behavioral, and academic outcomes in school (Boyd, 2012; Delisle, 2012; McConville, 2013; Toste, Heath, & Dellaire, 2010). Making time in the day to provide spontaneous character education using PCAT, which facilitates the use of praise and affirmative teacher-student relationships, is clearly worth the effort.

Don't Plan It: Be Spontaneous

Worthy of note in the aforementioned examples, the educators provided the PCAT in a spontaneous manner. As previously mentioned in this article, so much of character education in schools is derived from a preplanned program implemented in a reserved time slot. Or, students participate in preplanned assemblies or half-time at sporting events that have an emphasis on "good" character. While these tasks may exemplify what good character means and highlight students who exhibit it, these tasks are meant to relate to a whole group; they do not speak to an individual's sense of self as Chen (2013) and Ryan (2013) suggest is necessary. Instead, educators should capitalize on spontaneous, teachable moments that are impromptu and "not something you put in a lesson plan ... [they are] exquisitely timed" (Neuman & Roskos, 2012, 66). The benefit of teachable moments is they inherently relate to students' interests due to their unplanned, spontaneous nature often instigated by students. Therefore, educators have the opportunity to provide spontaneous character education in moments that already have students' attention and interest, which is an opportunity to positively influence students' thinking.

Stick With It: Be Persistent

Fourth, some students may appear unresponsive to educators who provide character education using PCAT, despite repeated efforts. Educators know students' perspectives and beliefs do not change immediately, regardless of the intensity of the effort put forth. Yet, as previously described, educators must continually focus on the positive in the negative of observed behaviors, believing that the social persuasion involved in this type of character education will eventually positively influence students' thinking. Therefore, teachers' consistent and persistent efforts to provide PCAT is at the heart of spontaneous character education.

Monitor It: Self-Reflection

Finally, if educators are committed to character education in any capacity, they need to reflect on how well they provide it. Herrell, Jordan, and Eby (2013) indicate educators must constantly recognize the need to evaluate their own teaching, especially as it relates to students needs and interests" (p. 3). Robert Marzano, a pioneer in the field of reflective practice in education, suggests that teachers should "conduct self-audits … [which involve] a retrospective examination of one's strengths and weaknesses" (Marzano, 2012, p. 14). Specifically related to this article, educators need to document how and when they provide character education using PCAT over time. By doing so, themes may emerge about the time of day PCAT is most often or least often provided and the most common or least common/nonexistent positive causal attributes provided by the educator, as well as students' immediate or delayed responses. The data from this type of reflective practice can be used to set short-term goals related to how and when to provide PCAT and which positive attributions could be provided with more or less frequency. For example, an educator can strive to provide two incidences of PCAT per day or 10 per week. Ideally, this simple, self-reflection process is shared with a colleague to provide accountability and spur professional growth. Figure 1 is an example of a table for this self-reflection process.

Cautions and Qualifications

Although spontaneous character education using PCAT is grounded in theoretical frameworks and academic literature, caution must be applied when investigating this approach. First, spontaneous character education using PCAT has no empirical evidence of its effectiveness. Without data to support this approach, it is not considered evidence-based, which is necessary for school-based applications. Yet, researchers are highly encouraged to study its effectiveness in small and varied settings in order to investigate how viability of this approach.

Second, caution should be applied when investigating spontaneous character education using PCAT because this approach is not a "one size fits all" method. Brophy (1981) indicates that individual students respond to praise differently and how they "mediate" its meaning (p. 27. For example, older students have the tendency to interpret praise as indicating low ability, when younger students often interpret praise as true. Thus, the praise statements used within this new approach to character education needs to be age-appropriate and culturally relevant.

Third, this same scholar indicates praise and academic achievement are not cause and effect, especially if praise is implemented ineffectively. Many factors can affect academic achievement; character education is just one of many factors. Finally, Huitt (2004a) in his review of literature and describing his position on character education states the most important factor in developing good character in students is the quality of the relationships among the school's faculty and adults in authority. In

Teacher Name: _____

Bank of Possible Positive Causal Attributions:

Citizenship, commitment, compassion, courage, diligence, effort, ethical, fairness, helpfulness, honesty, initiative, integrity, loyalty, perseverance, preparedness, respect, responsibility, self-control, self-discipline, sportsmanship, trustworthiness

Date	Student	Find It PCA witnessed	Provide It What was said to the student	Don't Plan It Where/How it took place	Notes (e.g., response of student – immediate or delayed; self- reflection)
Example: 10/16	Jayvon	Helpfulness	"You were helpful when you picked up Mason's book that dropped from his hands. That was cool."	Hall duty before lunch.	He smiled.
Most common PCA I find & provide:					
Other themes that emerge over time:					

FIGURE 1
Character Education using Positive Causal Attributions Training (PCAT): Teacher Self-Evaluation

essence, investigations of spontaneous character education using PCAT should be implemented with a measured tone.

IMPLICATIONS

Due to the current lack of empirical evidence using spontaneous character education using PCAT, there are several implications for future investigations. First, implementing such an approach to character education would be no small task for teachers. They would need to develop a highly sensitive "eye" for the general and particulars of human nature. Therefore, as suggested by DeRoche and Williams (1998), Milson (1999), and Ryan (1997), educator preparation programs (EPPs) would be an early and fitting place for such specific training. Many EPPs are under the demands of accrediting bodies that abide by the Interstate Teacher Assessment and Support Consortium (InTASC), which provides standards for teacher effectiveness. The InTASC standards require EPPs to train teacher candidates on critical dispositions (Council of Chief State School Officers, 2011), which are "habits of action and mind emanating from values and beliefs" (Ingles, 2014, p. 1). This mandate for EPPs of teaching "habits of action and mind" aligns with the precepts of spontaneous character education using PCAT where character is defined as acting on values. If teacher candidates become more aware of their own dispositions, they may be better able to identify their future students' dispositions prior to their first teaching position.

Second, "buy-in" to spontaneous character education using PCAT needs to start with administration, in particular principals. In their joint review of the literature in 2013, the National Association of Secondary Principals (NASSP) and the National Association of Elementary Principals (NAESP) purport that principals affect student learning, teacher retention, and the priorities of the school. And, Habegger (2008) suggests that amidst the varying roles principals play, creating and maintaining a positive school culture is imperative. While NASSP, NAESP, and Habegger indicate the responsibility of school culture and performance does not rest solely on the leadership of the principal, this role is often the most influential. Therefore, if spontaneous character education using PCAT would be implemented in schools, principals would need to embrace it for its impact to trickle down to teachers and students.

Third, teachers who implement spontaneous character education using PCAT would need added support from administration. Teachers today feel immense pressure in the classroom, especially related to improving test scores (Walker, 2014). Therefore, the implementation of this new approach to character education would need to be as seamless as possible and in a manner that does not feel like just "another thing to do." A seamless implementation may likely involve training using case study so teachers can develop an efficient "eye" for seeing values in action.

CONCLUSION

Educators play an essential role when implementing character education programs. Yet, the implementation of current character education programs remains in its own silo with weak effectiveness. Spontaneous character education using PCAT, though, offers an alternative to typical implementations. This new perspective and approach to character education draws positive attention to students' personal values in action. The difference from typical implementation practices and how spontaneous character education using PCAT might be implemented is students see their positive attributes as the cause of positive behaviors they demonstrate during unplanned, routine school-based tasks. In other words, students see at a moment's notice ways in which they act on controllable, unstable, positive causal attributions.

The large-scale impact of spontaneous character education might positively impact thousands of students' core values and consequent self-efficacy and achievement in much the same way as it impacted Tyler, the basketball player in the vignette. Immediately after Tyler received the PCAT, he hustled down the court and scored a basket. His contribution helped his team win the game in the final seconds. No doubt, Tyler's self-efficacy reached a new height during this particular game due to the PCAT he received. Using PCAT within a spontaneous education program could potentially have the same positive effect but on thousands of students. Imagine the effects of verbally and individually labeling each student in a district as *responsible, trustworthy, honest, ethical, persistent, compassionate, respectful,* and *self-disciplined* instead of *at-risk, below level, trouble maker,* and *bully*. Spontaneous character education using PCAT has the potential to offset students' maladaptive thinking perpetuated by in- and out-of-school stressors students experience. Spontaneously training students to think about why they enact goodness is definitely a strategy to score points toward a "win" in the school context and in the game of life.

REFERENCES

Bandura, A. (1977). Self-efficacy: Toward a unifying theory of behavioral change. *Psychological Review, 84*, 191–215. doi:10.1037/0033-295X.84.2.191

Bandura, A. (1995). *Self-efficacy in changing societies*. New York, NY: Cambridge University Press.

Benninga, J., Berkowitz, M., Kuehn, E., & Smith, K. (2006). Character and academics: What good schools do. *Phi Delta Kappan, 87*, 448–452.

Berkowitz, M., & Bier, M. (2005). *What works in character education: A research-driven guide for educators*. Washington, DC: Character Education Partnership.

Boyd, L. (2012, October). 5 myths about student discipline. *Educational Leadership*, 62–66.

Brophy, J. (1981). Teacher praise: A functional analysis. *Review of Educational Research, 51*(1), 5–32

Chen, Y.-L. (2013). A missing piece of the contemporary character education puzzle: The individualization of moral character. *Studies in Philosophy & Education, 32*(4), 345–360. doi:10.1007/s11217-012-9331-6

Cherne, J. (2009). *Effects of praise on student behavior in the classroom* (Doctoral dissertation). Retrieved September 28, 2015, from Dissertations & Theses: Full Text. (Publication No. AAT 3328300)

Chodkiewicz, A., & Boyle, C. (2014). Exploring the contribution of attribution retraining to student perceptions and the learning process. *Educational Psychology in Practice, 30*(1), 78–87.

Council of Chief State School Officers. (2011). *InTASC Model core teaching standards: A resource for state dialogue*. Retrieved from www.ccsso.org/documents/2011/intasc_model_core_teaching_standards_2011.pdf

Davis, D. (2006). Character education in America's public schools. *Journal of Church & State, 48*(1) 5–14.

Delisle, J. (2012) Reaching those we teach: The five Cs of student engagement. *Gifted Child Today, 35*(1), 62–67. doi: 10.1177/1076217511427513

DeRoche, E. F., & Williams, M. M. (1998). *Educating hearts and minds: A comprehensive character education framework*. Thousand Oaks, CA: Corwin Press.

Doll, B., Spies, R. A., LeClair, C. M., Kurien, S. A., Foley, B. P. (2010). Student perceptions of classroom learning environments: Development of the ClassMaps survey. *School Psychology Review, 39*(2), 203–218.

Dominguez, N., & Hager, M. (2013). Mentoring frameworks: Synthesis and critique. *International Journal of Mentoring and Coaching in Education, 2*(3), 171–188. doi:10.1108/IJMCE-03-2013-0014

Fulk, B., & Mastropieri, M. (1990). Training positive attitudes: I tried hard and did well! *Intervention in School Clinic, 26*, 79–83.

Graham, S., & Weiner, B. (1996). Theories and principles of motivation. In D. C. Berliner & R. Calfee (Eds.), *Handbook of educational psychology* (pp. 63–84). New York, NY: Macmillan.

Griggs, M., Gagnon, S., Huelsman, T. J., Kidder-Ashley, P., & Ballard, M. (2009). Student-teacher relationships matter: Moderating influences between temperament and preschool social competence. *Psychology in the Schools, 46*(6), 553–567.

Habegger, S. (2008). The principal's role in successful schools: Creating a positive school culture. *Principal*, 42–46. Retrieved from https://www.naesp.org/resources/1/Principal/2008/S-O_p42.pdf

Haynes, C., & Thomas, O. (2011). *Finding common ground: A guide to religious liberty in public schools*. Nashville, TN: First Amendment Center.

Herrell, A., Jordan, M., & Eby, J. (2013). *Teaching in the elementary school: A reflective action approach* (6th ed.). Boston, MA: Pearson.

Hill, E., Milliken, T., Goff, J., Clark, D., & Gagnon, R. (2015). Development and Implementation of CARE Now: A University, municipal recreational department, and public school collaborative model. *Journal of Park and Recreation Administration, 33*(3), 62–75.

Howes, C., Hamilton, C. E., Matheson, C. C. (1994). Children's relationships with peers: Differential associations with aspects of the teacher-child relationship. *Child Development, 65*, 253–263.

Huitt, W. (2004a). Moral and character development. *Educational Psychology Interactive.* Valdosta, GA: Valdosta State University. Retrieved from http://www.edpsycinteractive.org/morchr/morchr.html

Huitt, W. (2004b). Values. *Educational Psychology Interactive.* Valdosta, GA: Valdosta State University. Retrieved from http://www.edpsycinteractive.org/topics/affect/values.html#Action

Hyungsook, K. (2014). Socially engaged art practice and character education: Understanding others through visual art. *International Journal of Education through Art, 10*(1), 55–69.

Ingles, S. (2014). Developing critical skills: Interactive exercises for pre-service teachers. Dubuque, IA: Kendall Hunt.

Katilmis, A., Eksi, H., & Ozturk, C. (2011). Efficiency of social studies integrated character education program. *Educational Sciences: Theory & Practice, 11*(2), 854–859.

Kozminsky, E., & Kozminsky, L. (2003). Improving motivation through dialogue. *Educational Leadership, 61*(1), 50–54.

Lickona, T. (1991). *Education for character: how our schools can teach respect and responsibility.* New York, NY: Bantam Books.

Margolis, H., & McCabe, P. (2004). Self-efficacy: A key to improving the motivation of struggling learners. *The Clearing House, 77*(6), 241–249.

Marshall, J., Caldwell, S., & Foster, J. (2011). Moral education the CHARACTERplus way. *Journal of Moral Education, 40*, 51–72.

Marzano, R., Marzano, J., & Pickering, D. (2003). *Classroom management that works.* New York, NY: McGraw-Hill.

McConville, A. (2013). Teaching as a cultural and relationship-based activity. *Mind, Brain, and Education, 7*(3), 170–176.

Milson, A. J. (1999). The perceptions of social studies teacher educators regarding character education (Doctoral dissertation. University of Georgia, 1999). Dissertation Abstracts International, 60(05), 1517. (UMI No. 9928968)

National Association of Secondary Principals & National Association of Elementary School Principals. (2013). *Leadership matters: What the research says about the importance of principal leadership,* 1–12. Reston, VA and Alexandria VA: Authors. Retrieved from http://www.naesp.org/sites/default/files/LeadershipMatters.pdf

Niemic, R., Rashid, R., & Spinella, M. (2012). Strong mindfulness: Integrating mindfulness and character strengths. *Journal of Mental Health Counseling, 34*(3), 240–253.

Neuman, S., & Roskos, K. (2012). More than teachable moments: Enhancing vocabulary instruction in your classroom. *The Reading Teacher, 66*(1), 63–67. doi:10.1002/TRTR.01104

Pearl, R. (1982). LD children's attributions for success and failure: A replication with a labeled LD sample. *Learning Disability Quarterly, 5,* 173–176.

Power, F. (2014). With liberty and justice for all: Character education for America's future. *Journal of Character Education 10*(1), 31–36.

Robertson, J. S. (2000). Is attribution training a worthwhile classroom intervention for K–12 student with learning difficulties? *Educational Psychology Review, 12*, 111–134.

Roso, C. (2013). Culture and character education in a Jewish day school: A case study of life and experiences. *Journal of Research on Christian Education, 22*, 30–51.

Russell, W., & Waters, S. (2014). Developing character in middle school students: A cinematic approach. *The Clearing House, 87*, 161–167.

Ryan, K. (1997). The missing link's missing link. *Journal of Education, 179*(2), 81–90.

Ryan, K. (2013). The failure of modern character education. *Spanish Journal of Education, 254,* 141–146.

Ryan, K., & Bohlin, K. (1999) *Building character in Schools.* San Francisco, CA: Jossey-Bass.

Schunk, D. H., & Ertmer, P. A. (1999). Self-regulatory processes during computer skill acquisition: Goal and self-evaluative influences. *Journal of Educational Psychology, 91*, 251–260.

Scott, J. (1996). Self-efficacy: A key to literacy learning. *Reading Horizons, 36*(3), 195–213.

Shields, D. (2011). Character as the aim of education. *Phi Delta Kappan, 92*(8), 48–53.

Simonsen, B., Myers, D., & DeLuca, C. (2010). Teaching teachers to use prompts, opportunities to respond, and specific praise. *Teacher Education and Special Education, 33*(4), 300–318.

Social and Character Development Research Consortium. (2010). *Efficacy of schoolwide programs to promote social and character development and reduce problem behavior in elementary school children* (NCER 2011–2001). Washington, DC: National Center for Education Research, Institute of Education Sciences, U.S.

Department of Education. Retrieved from http://ies.ed.gov/ncer/pubs/20112001/

Sojourner, R. (2014). It's unanimous: Effective character education is not quick or superficial, and it begins with caring relationships. *Journal of Character Education, 10*(1), 69–75.

Sugai, G. (2007). Promoting behavioral competence in schools: A commentary on exemplary practices. *Psychology in the Schools, 44*(1), 113–118. doi:10.1002/pits.20210

Toste, J., Heath, N., & Dallaire, L. (2010). Perceptions of classroom working alliance and student performance. *The Alberta Journal of Educational Research, 56*(4), 371–387.

U.S. Department of Education. (2007). *What Works Clearing House topic report: Character education.* Retrieved from http://files.eric.ed.gov/fulltext/ED497054.pdf

Weiner, B. (1985). An attributional theory of achievement motivation and emotion. *Psychological Review, 92*(4), 548–573.

Weiner, B. (1986). *An attributional theory of motivation and emotion.* New York, NY: Springer-Verlag.

THE RELATIONSHIP BETWEEN ATTACHMENT AND GRIT IN LOWER INCOME ADOLESCENTS

Toni Mandelbaum
Private Practice

This research intended to further our understanding of the construct grit, defined as maintaining persistence and passion when pursuing long-term goals (Duckworth et al., 2007). The study had 2 aims: first to confirm a correlation between the construct of grit and an individual's attachment style and second, to examine this relationship in high school seniors from lower socioeconomic backgrounds. The study was conducted on 42 lower socioeconomic, 18-year-old high school seniors at 3 different school sites. Self-report measures were used in addition to a story-telling attachment measure. The results of this exploratory study provided further evidence that there is a connection between attachment and grit. Low-income high school students with insecure attachment patterns were found to be less gritty.

INTRODUCTION

Each year in the United States, close to 1.3 million students do not finish high school. In fact, reports indicate that only 78.6% of those who enter high school ultimately graduate (Alliance For Excellent Education, 2010; Stillwell & Sable, 2013) and 15% of those between 18 and 24 years of age do not have a high school diploma (U.S. Census Bureau, 2004, 2006). Those from lower income backgrounds as well as minority students are even less likely to successfully complete high school and then continue toward a college degree, often in spite of high achievement during their early school years (Leonhardt, 2013). This disparity in educational completion is linked to the growing economic inequality in this country (Putnam, 2015). Increasingly, researchers are viewing character skills, or noncognitive skills, such as diligence, perseverance, self-control, and grit (Heckman & Rubinstein, 2001; Reeves, Venator, & Howard, 2014; Sroufe, 2005; Tough, 2012) as equally if not more relevant than cognitive skills in understanding this discrepancy. Knowledge of how to engender these skills may help our ability to address the growing economic and educational gaps in our country.

This research aims to further our understanding of one of these noncognitive skills: grit, defined as maintaining persistence and passion in the pursuit of a long-term goal

• **Correspondence concerning this article should be addressed to:** Toni Mandelbaum, toni.mandelbaum@gmail.com

Journal of Character Education, Volume 14(1), 2018, pp. 59–74
Copyright © 2018 Information Age Publishing, Inc.

(Duckworth et al., 2007; Duckworth & Gross, 2014). Past research has focused on its definition and its correlates (Eskreis-Winkler, Shulman, Beal, & Duckworth, 2014). However, there is still much to be learned about the factors that influence an individual's grittiness. These authors suggest that the attachment bond, a construct that is underresearched with respect to grit, may be a critical component of this character skill.

Past research highlights the importance of the attachment relationship to optimal development. Alan Sroufe's (2005) longitudinal data provides strong support for the notion that a secure attachment relationship can engender better self-regulation, help develop effective coping mechanisms, and improve overall successful functioning, all qualities correlated with grit (Duckworth et al., 2007). Levy and Steele (2011) explored the attachment bond as a likely underpinning of grit and found a positive relationship between the constructs. However, their survey study was conducted on an economically diverse sample in which ages ranged from 18–87, and relied solely on self-report measures. This study used narrative attachment instruments as well as self-report measures and focused solely on lower income high school seniors, a population that has not yet been studied. This research aims to both confirm a connection between attachment and grit and to establish this connection in a lower-income, adolescent population.

Why Study Low-Income High School Seniors?

Low income high school seniors are seen as an ideal demographic group in which to study the relationship between attachment and grit for the following reasons. First, there is little research examining how adolescents' levels of grit are affected by living in lower income neighborhoods. There is evidence to support the fact that cognitive development in children may be impacted by the stress of living in poverty. For instance, in a lower-income sample, lower executive function ability as well as IQ at age 3 was associated with higher levels of salivary cortisol, an indicator of a stress response (Blair et al., 2011). Furthermore, Duckworth, Kim, and Tsukayama (2013) found that deleterious life events encountered by school-aged children can negatively affect cognitive abilities such as inhibitory control and attention shifting or flexibility, abilities related to grit. However, the authors are not aware of other studies examining grit in adolescents from lower income areas. This research aims to contribute to the literature on this possible connection.

Secondly, high school seniors are in their late adolescence, a time of great vulnerability. Adolescence, or the period of transition to adulthood, has been called "demographically dense" (Rindfuss, 1991), or a time at which many potentially stressful life stage events often occur. This includes completing school, leaving home, and becoming economically viable. Epidemiological data shows that adolescence, as a phase of life, is associated with profound risks such as alcohol and drug abuse, self-harm, interpersonal violence, and legal difficulties for disadvantaged adolescents (Jensen & Nutt, 2015; Steinberg, 2014). In addition to the many life transitions occurring, adolescents are also undergoing many physiological changes. The brain is not yet fully developed and continues developing into early adulthood (Jensen & Nutt, 2015; Steinberg, 2014). Correlates of brain development, such as maturation of the overall neuroendocrine system, also continue to be experience-dependent during this time. Thus, adolescents may both experience more stress during this life phase and be less robust in their ability to manage stress in pursuit of longer term aspirations and goals. From an attachment perspective, it is a period of evolution where the adolescent moves away from receiving care and toward becoming an adult and being able to provide care (Allen, 2008). During this time of transition, adolescents very much need attachment figures to function as a secure base. Therefore, attachment security or insecurity may feature in how an adolescent persists toward meeting long-term goals.

LITERATURE REVIEW

Grit

Duckworth and her colleagues view grit as one of the factors critical to achievement and educational success (Duckworth et al., 2007; Duckworth & Quinn, 2009). According to Duckworth et al., individuals who are gritty maintain passion and perseverance when working toward long-term goals, often in spite of obstacles and setbacks (Duckworth & Gross, 2014). Research has corroborated this definition. Higher levels of grit predicted completion of a cadet summer training course above physical fitness, academic grades, or a leadership score (Duckworth et al., 2007). Gritty high school students were more likely to complete high school; gritty soldiers were more likely to finish three weeks of a difficult selection course; gritty sales people were more likely to exhibit job retention long-term; and gritty males were more likely to stay married (Eskreis-Winkler, Shulman, Beal, & Duckworth, 2014). Furthermore, National Spelling Bee finalists with more grit practiced more and therefore advanced to further rounds than their less gritty counterparts. Teachers who were grittier were more likely to finish the school year and also performed better than less gritty teachers (Robertson-Kraft & Duckworth, 2014). More grit predicted higher GPAs, more extracurricular activities, and less television watching among middle and high school students (Duckworth & Quinn, 2009) and has been related to attaining higher education levels, to fewer career changes, and to undergraduates at a competitive university earning higher GPAs (Duckworth et al., 2007). Thus, better understanding grit's underlying factors as well as the processes necessary to create it may help to improve adolescents' chances of success.

Adolescent and Adult Attachment

John Bowlby (1973), the originator of attachment theory, defined an attachment bond as a relationship that serves a dual function: that of providing a safe haven, or a place of comfort, during times of threat and distress and a "secure base" (Ainsworth et al., 1978) from which an individual springboards to explore the environment when feeling unthreatened (Bowlby, 1973). A child organizes his or her behaviors within this relationship in order to assure himself of safety. A caregiver is either available or unavailable to a child. Based on a caregiver's responsiveness, the child develops paradigms, or cognitive representations, of the self in relationships and these representations guide future interactions throughout the lifecycle.

Bowlby proposed the attachment bond to be a universal need, such that all human beings are born predisposed to forming this relationship. However, not all people form the same attachment bond. Individual differences exist and these differences are based on the unique transactional experiences occurring within the attachment dyad. Bowlby divided the attachment bond into two types: secure and insecure. Later, Mary Ainsworth, Bowlby's colleague (1978), expanded the classifications into three: secure, resistant/ambivalent, and avoidant. In the Strange Situation, a laboratory study, infants who are securely attached are able to tolerate brief separations from a caregiver, showing signs of missing the caregiver during separation and actively greeting the caregiver when reunited. Resistant/ambivalent infants are preoccupied with the parent throughout separation and are unable to settle down when the parent returned. Avoidantly attached infants focus on the environment during separation and show little emotion toward the caregiver upon reunion (Ainsworth & Bowlby, 1991). Mary Main introduced a fourth classification, that of disorganized attachment (Main & Solomon, 1990). Here, there was no observable pattern in the child's reactions to the separation or to the reunion. These four behavior patterns translate into adult attachment styles.

The field of attachment has different conceptualizations and evaluations of individual adolescent and adult attachment. In 1988, Hazan and Shaver (1987) initiated the study of adult romantic attachment. Social psychologists, building on this research, have concluded that adult attachment consists of two dimensions: Anxiety and Avoidance (Shaver & Mikulincer, 2002). Those with attachment anxiety fear abandonment or rejection, feel excessively upset when a partner is unavailable, have an overwhelming need for approval, and use hyperactivating strategies to negotiate their distress. Those with attachment avoidance fear intimacy and relying on others, are overly independent and self-reliant, and utilize deactivating affect-regulation strategies to deal with distress (Shaver & Mikulincer, 2009). Bartholomew and Horowitz (1991) furthered the study of adolescent and adult attachment by postulating a four category classification of attachment styles existing along the two-dimensional space defined by attachment-related anxiety and avoidance. These four types can be conceptualized as a quadrant, where those with high attachment anxiety (termed resistant/ambivalent in the Strange Situation) or avoidance (termed avoidant in the Strange Situation) are understood as being insecurely attached, those with low levels of attachment anxiety and avoidance are assumed to be securely attached, while those with both high levels of anxiety and avoidance are seen as fearfully attached (similar to what is termed disorganized in the Strange Situation) (Shaver & Mikulincer, 2008). This line of thinking has led to the development of many self-report instruments measuring adolescent and adult attachment patterns.

Recently, another thrust in adolescent and adult attachment research examines the secure base script. As stated above, an attachment relationship provides a secure base from which to explore the environment and a safe haven to return to in times of distress. Lately, researchers have hypothesized that an individual's heuristic that is developed within the attachment bond is organized or represented as a secure base script. This theory is based on Bretherton's (1987) work suggesting that experiences are encoded as cognitive structures, or summaries of commonalities in events that occur in particular situations. These summaries result in a script, or a map that guides expectations and behavior in the future (Waters & Waters, 2006). With respect to attachment, these secure base scripts are thought to be the cognitive building blocks of attachment representations (Coppola, Vaughn, Cassibba, & Constantini, 2006). The scripts are assumed to be organized around the following three central affect-regulating strategies: the recognition and manifestation of distress, engaging and resolution-seeking, and soliciting support (Shaver & Mikulincer, 2002). Thus, when a stressor is encountered, presumably the secure base script is activated and the individual will expect script-consistent behavior in close relationships. Also, the individual will use the script to organize his or her reactions to the stressor (Waters & Waters, 2006). Hence, secure individuals feel confident that either they can rely on attachment figures for support or that they can solve their own distress. Insecurely attached individuals will be uncertain of the attachment figure's availability and will doubt his or her ability to resolve the issue at hand. Research supports the fact that early caregiving experiences manifest in individual differences in secure base script knowledge and that the script assessment can measure this abstraction (Steele et al., 2014). Secure base scripts are linked with attachment in adolescents and adults (Dykas, Woodhouse, Cassidy, & Waters, 2006; Waters & Rodrigues-Doolabh, 2001) and measures such as the Adolescent Script Assessment are based on this understanding of attachment patterns.

Theoretical Link Between Attachment and Grit

As stated previously, grit is defined as maintaining passion and perseverance when working toward long-term goals. Meeting these goals often entails competently responding to setbacks, adversity, and failures (Duck-worth et al., 2007). Presumably such stamina requires effectively self-regulating the stress and negative emotions that may ensue from the encountered difficulties. According to Eisen-berg and colleagues (2014), self-regulation is defined as the modulation of emotional, behavioral, and attentional responses in the service of a desired goal. In fact, grit and self-regulatory capacities are inextricably linked. Grit has been found to be highly cor-related with self-control ($r = .63$, $p < .001$) (Duckworth et al., 2007; Duckworth & Selig-man, 2017), a construct involving the capacity to control, inhibit or override thoughts, emo-tions, impulses and behaviors in order to max-imize future gains MacCann & Roberts, 2010; Tangney, Baumeister, & Boone, 2004) and to correlate with aspects of self-regulation (Rojas et al., 2012; Wolters Y Hussain, 2015), a facet of self-control.

As stated above, this research was based on the supposition that attachment and grit are related constructs. According to attachment theory, children learn to self-regulate through caregiver-child interaction (Diamond & Fagundes, 2008; Kopp, 1982). Indeed, research has confirmed a strong link between dyadic regulation within the attachment rela-tionship in infancy and later self-regulation functioning in childhood into adulthood (Sroufe et al., 2005). From a theoretical per-spective, the attachment system can be viewed as a psychobiological regulator of stress whereby the child utilizes a "safe haven" to achieve homeostasis and from there, a "secure base" to launch from and continue with explo-ration. Bowlby defined three interlocking behavioral systems; the attachment system, the exploratory system, and the fear system. The activation of the fear system disables the exploration system and enables the attachment system. A frightened child seeks proximity to an attachment figure (attachment system) and temporarily curtails exploration until he or she feels secure once more. Activation of the attachment system usually instigates behaviors to try to either reestablish contact with the

caregiver or to ensure the attachment figure's availability (Kobak et al., 2006). The availabil-ity, or the cognitive appraisal of a caregiver's availability, is crucial in a child's feeling securely attached (Bowlby, 1973; Kobak, 1999). It is also essential in a child's develop-ing ultimate autonomy. According to Ainsworth, the exploration system allows the learning process to occur (Ainsworth et al., 1978). A child learns self-regulation through repeated interactions with an available care-giver who encourages exploration. We hypoth-esize that with the development of self-regulation comes the capacity to persist and persevere through adversity and to work toward meeting long-term goals, or to be gritty. To summarize, this research, though exploratory in nature, is intended to add to the growing body of research examining how to potentially enable change and improve pas-sion, persistence, and perseverance in low-income adolescents when pursuing long-term goals. Understanding the connection between attachment and grit in a disadvan-taged population of high school seniors could perhaps contribute to efforts addressing the socioeconomic gaps in school achievement and completion.

HYPOTHESES

The following were hypothesized:

1. There is an association between attach-ment pattern (operationalized in this study as Attachment-related Anxiety, Attach-ment-related Avoidance, and ASA score) and Total Grit Score, where those who are less anxious and avoidant and those who are more secure have more grit.
2. Both factors that comprise Total Grit, Grit Consistency and Grit Perseverance, will correlate with attachment pattern (Attach-ment-related Anxiety, Attachment-related Avoidance, and ASA score), where those who are less anxious and avoidant, and

those who are more secure have more consistency of interest and more perseverance.

METHOD

School Facts

1. **High school in Northeast Philadelphia:** This high school has Title 1 status, meaning that as per "Title 1, Part A of the Elementary and Secondary Education act, as amended (ESEA) provides financial assistance is provided to local educational agencies (LEAs) and schools with high numbers or high percentages of children from low-income families to help ensure that all children meet challenging state academic standards (http://paschoolperformance.org/Profile/6787)." One hundred percent of enrolled students are economically disadvantaged. Of the 1,210 students enrolled, .17% are American Indian/Alaskan Native, 1.24% Asian, 52.64% Black or African American, 33.64% Hispanic, and 9.5% are White. Females make up 42.64% of the student body and males make up 57.36%. For the school year of 2013–2014, the dropout rate from this high school was 9.5%, while the graduation rate was 60.10%. The high school's academic performance score is a 38%, based on a range of scores from 0 to 100. This is a number based on calculations of data elements of standardized test scores. The calculations are a weighted average of test scores across 17 factors. The details can be found on the following website: http://paschoolperformance.org/Profile/6787.

2. **High school in Camden, New Jersey.** This high school is a Christian-based, private school in Camden, New Jersey, whose mission is to "equip Camden children and young adults with the skills necessary for academic achievement, life management, spiritual growth, and Christian leadership." Entrance is based on grades and an entrance exam that mea-

sures math, reading, and vocabulary comprehension. Those who are more than three levels below grade level are not accepted. The average tuition is $170 per month. Tuition is scale-based and depends on parental income as well as number of people in a household. The average reported income for families of students in this high school was $28,600 and the median income was $23,100. In 2013–2014, there were 43 students attending the high school, 44.44% males and 55.56% females. Of the 8 seniors enrolled, 100% graduated. Fifty percent of students are Black/African American individuals and 50% are Hispanic. As this is a private school, they do not have an academic performance score.

3. **Charter school in Northeast Philadelphia.** This charter school was founded in 1999 by a coalition of educators and community residents committed to creating a high performing middle and high school for the students of the Kensington neighborhood. Of the student body, 77% are Hispanic, 20% are Black, 2% are White, and 1% are two or more races. Fifty-two percent of the student body is female, while 48% is male.

Participants

Participants were 42 high-school seniors from three different school programs, all serving lower socioeconomic neighborhoods. Of the 42 participants, 28 (66.67%) were male and 14 (33.33%) were female. The participants' ages ranged from 18 to 20, with 25 (59.52%) 18-year-olds, 14 (33.33%) 19-year-olds, and three (7.14%) 20-year-olds. The mean age was 18.48. The sample included 12 (28.57%) Hispanic individuals, 23 (54.76%) Black/African Americans, 2 (4.76%) White/Caucasians, and 5 (11.90%) undeclared. Twenty-one (50%) of the participants lived in a two-parent household, 18 (42.86%) lived in a single-parent household, 2 (4.76%) lived without parents, and 1 (2.38%) had other living arrangements.

In terms of high schools attended, 9 (21.43%) students attended a high school in Northeast Philadelphia and 27 (64.29%) were enrolled in a program within that high school designed for those who had dropped out of school and then returned. This is an online, teacher-facilitated program primarily designed to help undercredited students work toward high school graduation. Two (4.76%) students attended a school in Camden, NJ, and 4 (9.52%) students attended a charter school in Northeast Philadelphia. The participation rates were very different. The school in Northeast Philadelphia had 1,210 students enrolled, as compared to the school in Camden, which had a total of 8 seniors. This explains the difference in participation rates between these two schools. Those from the Charter School participated only toward the end of data collection. Thus, the researchers did not have time to allow for more participants at this site. Twenty (47.62%) participants were unsure of their grade point average (GPA). There was a large range of grade point averages for the 22 (52.38%) subjects who reported their GPA, with the lowest average being .4 and the highest being 3.4. The GPA average of those who reported their grades was 2.60. Only three participants (7.14%) had SAT scores to report, two of 1440 and one of 1190, all out of 2400.

PROCEDURE

To recruit subjects, flyers were posted at each site on multiple bulletin boards in visible locations. The researcher also spoke to several classes about the research study and passed around a sign-up sheet with different time slots available for those who expressed interest in participating. Interested participants who saw the flyers that had been posted either signed up in a time-slot on a sheet next to the flyer or contacted the researcher in person or by phone and asked to participate in the study. Those who heard about the study through word of mouth personally approached the researcher and asked to participate in this study.

Data was gathered between March and June of 2014. Each subject completed the Adolescent Script Assessment (ASA) as well as self-report measures, including another attachment measure and a measure of grit. A researcher sat with each subject as he or she completed the questionnaires and in most cases, due to varying literacy levels, read the questionnaires to the subjects and then recorded their answers. The stories told during the ASA were audio-recorded. Because there was a researcher present for each participant, there were no questions that were left blank. It took approximately 1 to 1½ hours for each participant to fill in self-report forms and to tell stories. Each subject was given a $40 Amazon gift card for participation in the research.

Measures

Two different attachment measures were used: the ASA and the ECR-S:

1. **ASA**

   a. **Administration:** The assessment is designed to elicit attachment-related stories from adolescents. Subjects were presented with five laminated cards, each with a different story title. On each card were twelve prompt words. Subjects were asked to construct stories using these words. Girls were asked to complete stories entitled "The Party" and "Acne," using their mother as a character in these stories, and "Studying for an Exam" and "The Tennis Match," using their father as a character for these stories. Boys were asked to complete the same stories with the same instructions, except "Acne" was replaced with "The Haircut." Each of the four stories was recorded using an iPod for later verbatim transcription.

   b. **Scoring:** Each ASA was transcribed and then coded. Two coders were used per ASA to ensure interrater reliability. Both coders had successfully completed reliability training for the ASA. Scores were assigned for each story. Once the coders had scores for each story, they averaged the secure base script knowledge scores across all four stories to obtain a single composite score.

Narratives were coded using the method developed by Waters and Rodrigues-Doolabh (2001). They were scored on a 7-point scale. A prototypic secure base script uses the prompt words to describe a rich interplay between main characters and a sequence of events where exploration is encouraged and distress is effectively resolved. The highest score (7) is given to passages with extensive secure base script organization and a high degree of elaboration. The lowest score (1) is assigned to passages where prompt words are used in a haphazard way, with no secure base content (Waters & Rodrigues-Doolabh, 2001). In this sample, scores ranged from 1.06 to 5.06.

c. Psychometric Properties: Because this measure was recently developed, psychometric properties are still being ascertained. The ASA for adults has been shown to have adequate reliability and both construct and convergent validity have been established (Waters & Waters, 2006; Steele et al., 2014) (

2. **Experiences in Close Relationships Scale -Short Form (ECR-S)**

a. Description: The ECR-S is a 12-item, self-report questionnaire adapted from the ECR (Brennan, Clark, & Shaver, 1998) by Wei and colleagues (2007). The scale measures two relatively orthogonal continuous dimensions of attachment labeled Anxiety (6 items) and Avoidance (6 items). Respondents evaluate statements such as "It helps to turn to my romantic partner in times of need" on a scale from 1 ("strongly disagree") to 7 ("strongly agree"). Higher scores on either subscale indicate higher levels of either attachment avoidance or anxiety. In this sample, scores for attachment-related anx-

iety ranged from 1.00 to 6.67, while scores for attachment-related avoidance ranged from 1.17 to 6.17.

b. Psychometric properties: The ECR-S is based on the ECR, a 36-item questionnaire, whose psychometric properties have been well established (Brennan et al., 1998; Shaver & Mikulincer, 2002). The ECR-S has been shown to be a reliable and valid measure, possessing stable factor structure, adequate internal consistency, test-retest reliability, and construct validity (Wei et al., 2007).

3. **Grit-S**

a. Description: The Grit-S is an 8-item, self-report scale developed by Angela Duckworth and colleagues (Duckworth & Quinn, 2009) to measure grit, defined as perseverance, tenacity, and passion for goals. A maximum score is 5, indicating high grit and the lowest score on the scale is 1, or not at all gritty. In this sample, scores for grit ranged from 2.25 to 4.50.

The Grit-S is confirmed as a two-factor model where "consistency of interest" and "perseverance of effort" both load onto grit (Duckworth & Quinn, 2009; Duckworth, 2016). Scores for each factor were calculated. In this sample, scores for "consistency of interest" ranged from 1.00 to 4.50 and scores for "perseverance of effort" ranged from 2.75 to 5.00.

b. Psychometric properties: The Grit-S has been shown to have internal consistency, test-retest stability, consensual validity with informant-report versions, and predictive validity (Duckworth & Quinn, 2009).

RESULTS

Correlational Analyses

The means, standard deviations, and Pearson correlations (evaluated with two-tailed significance tests) among the main variables of the study are shown in Table 1.

TABLE 1

Means, Standard Deviations, and Correlations Among Study Variables

Measure	1	2	3	4	5	6
1. Attachment Avoidance		.142	−.317*	−.326*	−.242	−.273
2. Attachment Anxiety			.063	−.582**	−.512**	−.463**
3. Adolescent Script Assessment				.116	−.009	.264
4. Grit					.912**	.697**
5. Grit Consistency						.347*
6. Grit Perseverance						
Mean	3.048	3.563	3.022	3.619	3.089	4.1429
SD	1.252	1.112	.891	.636	.950	.585

Note: *$p < .05$. **$p < .01$.

TABLE 2

Predicting Grit From Attachment Strategies

Variable	Unstandardized B	SE B	Standardized β	t	Sig
Attachment Anxiety	−.313	.072	−.547	−4.362	.000
Attachment Avoidance	−.126	.064	−.248	−1.981	.055

Note: *$p < .05$.

Hypothesis 1

As can be seen in Table 1, Attachment-related Anxiety correlated negatively with Total Grit ($r(40) = −.582$, $p < .01$), as did Attachment-related Avoidance ($r(40) = −.326$, $p < .05$). There was not a significant relationship between Secure Base Script Knowledge, as evidenced by the ASA scores, and Total Grit.

Because Attachment-related Anxiety and Attachment-related Avoidance were slightly, although not significantly correlated with each other, an ordinary least squares regression analysis was performed, where the two attachment variables were regressed onto Total Grit. (As there was not a significant relationship between Total Grit and Secure Base Script Knowledge, the latter variable was not included in the regression model.) The results are shown in Table 2.

Attachment-related Anxiety had significant unique effects on Total Grit, while the effect that Attachment-related Avoidance had on Total Grit was not significant. The model was statistically significant, $F(2,39) = 12.97$, $p < .001$, and the two attachment variables together accounted for 39.9% of the variance in Total Grit ($R = .632$). For Attachment-related Anxiety, $β = −.547$, $p < .001$; for Attachment-related Avoidance, $β = −.248$, $p = .055$. Thus, Attachment-related Anxiety seems to have a negative impact on Total Grit.

Hypothesis 2

As can be seen in Table 1, Attachment-related Anxiety correlated negatively with Grit Consistency ($r(40) = −.512$, $p < .01$) and with Grit Perseverance ($r(40) = −.463$, $p < .01$). There were no significant relationships between Attachment-related Avoidance and Grit Consistency or Attachment-related Avoidance and Grit Perseverance. Furthermore, there were no significant relationships between Secure Base Script Knowledge and Grit Consistency or with Grit Perseverance.

Note about the attachment measures: As can be seen in Table 1, Attachment-related Anxiety and the ASA were not significantly correlated with each other, but Attachment-related Avoidance and the ASA were significantly negatively correlated with one another ($r(40) = -.317, p < .05$), meaning there was an inverse relationship between Attachment-related avoidance, as measured by the ECR-S, and Secure Base Attachment, as measured by the ASA.

DISCUSSION

This study provides further evidence for a relationship between attachment patterns and grit. More specifically, the research supports this connection in a lower income high school senior sample. Results indicate that those who are insecurely attached are likely to be "less gritty". In this study, attachment anxiety and attachment avoidance were both significantly negatively correlated with overall grit. Conversely, those who were more securely attached were more gritty and those who were more fearfully attached were less gritty. This endorses the idea that attachment bonds and the attachment patterns that develop within these relationships can affect an individual's ability to persevere over the long haul, often despite obstacles or setbacks that may be encountered.

The relationship between attachment patterns and grit, as shown by regression analyses, provides further support for a connection between attachment patterns and an individual's level of grit. Because this was a cross-sectional and not a longitudinal study, a potential causal relationship between attachment and grit was not testable. However, the results indicate that this is an avenue worth pursuing in the future.

As far as grit's two factors, Grit Consistency and Grit Perseverance were inversely related to Attachment-related anxiety. Thus,

results support the notion that attachment anxiety may impact both factors of grit: passion and perseverance in adolescents. This exploratory study not only provides evidence for a connection between how much grit a disadvantaged adolescent possesses and that individual's attachment patterns, but suggests that attachment patterns may be related to an adolescent's consistency of interest as well as his or her perseverance when working toward meeting long-term goals. Of note, two different attachment measures were used and different results were obtained with each attachment measure. Furthermore, Attachment-related Anxiety was not correlated with the ASA, while Attachment-related Avoidance was negatively related. The ASA focuses on the secure base relationship and the kinds of expectations an individual has from his or her caregivers. With the script approach, those who tell narratives with supportive caregivers are thought to be secure and those who tell narratives with unsupportive caregivers are thought to be insecure. This is in contrast to the ECR-S which is a self-report measure that assesses an individual's own understanding of their characteristic feelings and behavioral tendencies in close relationships, mostly concerning romantic relationships. Thus, the measures are examining different aspects of attachment. This data showed a correlation between Attachment-related Anxiety and Attachment-related Avoidance and conversely a positive relationship with Secure Base Script Knowledge (as measured by the ASA) and Total Grit, but not between Secure Base Script Knowledge, as measured by the ASA, and Total Grit. Perhaps grit and the ECR-S are measuring similar dimensions of self-regulatory capacities and self-perception in relationships, while the ASA is measuring an individual's perceived security in caregiving relationships, which in and of itself may not translate to grit.

The fact that Attachment-related Anxiety and Attachment-related Avoidance yield differing results in this study may be because the ECR-S is measuring different self-regulatory capacities. As stated, Attachment-related Anxiety is highly significantly correlated with overall Grit, as well as with the two Grit sub-scales: Grit Consistency and Grit Persever-ance. Attachment-related Avoidance, however, correlates significantly with Total Grit, but not with either of the subscales. To reiterate, individuals who are gritty maintain a consistent interest over a long period of time and are able to persevere toward meeting long-term goals related to this interest, often in spite of obstacles and setbacks. It is likely that those with grit are able to utilize effective reg-ulatory strategies to better negotiate the affect dysregulation that may occur with encountered setbacks. As stated above, those who are anx-iously attached tend to utilize hyperactivating strategies and those who are avoidantly attached typically employ deactivating strate-gies when feeling dysregulated. Hyperactivat-ing strategies consist of heightening emotion and increasing efforts to elicit attention, while deactivating strategies are developed in order to minimize emotion and minimize the attach-ment relationship (Cassidy, 1994). The results of this study suggest that hyperactivating strat-egies may interfere with maintaining a per-sistent interest and persevering when pursuing long-term goals, while deactivating strategies may actually be more in line with what is required to maintain consistent interest and perseverance over the long haul. Perhaps feel-ing flooded with emotion is more detrimental to pursuing long-term goals as compared to the shutting down of emotion, which may help with being able to persist. This is an area for future research. Attachment-related Anxiety's not being related to the ASA, in contrast to Attachment-related Avoidance can possibly be explained by story-telling styles. Perhaps those who are avoidantly attached tell stories that are less developed and have less secure base knowledge exhibited in their stories, while those who are anxiously attached, as measured by the ECR-S, may not exhibit their attach-ment insecurity in relation to their caregivers, but only in relation to their feelings with regards to romantic relationships. While these hypotheses may explain the different findings,

an alternative explanation is that the stories told by this particular sample were not always adequate and the coders expressed difficulty with coding because of the quality of some of the stories. Several subjects in this sample were not proficient readers and were inexperi-enced with telling stories and both of these fac-tors may have contributed to insufficient stories. The ASA is a new measure that may need further development with low-income samples.

Limitations

There were several limitations to this study. Firstly, the sample size is small and therefore null findings may be due to low power and not disconfirmations of hypotheses. Secondly, the sample is fairly homogenous, given that the sample was only composed of low-income, high school seniors. The results, though signif-icant, are therefore not generalizable. Thirdly, the sample may have been inherently biased when measuring grit. The 27 students that were enrolled in the program for returning stu-dents had already demonstrated grit as they were tenaciously working toward their degree instead of discontinuing high school. Many of these students had dropped out and then returned to high school and many were in dan-ger of dropping out, but were instead persever-ing toward graduation.

In terms of the measurements used, self-report measures can be problematic due to subject reporting biases. In this sample in par-ticular, many were illiterate and had the ques-tions read to them. This could have further biased the subjects' responses as they may have had response bias by seeking to please the interviewer. The coefficient reliability of the ECR-10 for this sample was adequate, but far below what is usual. This is potentially due to a misinterpretation of a double negative in one of the questions. The fact that most in the sam-ple may have misinterpreted double negatives casts doubt on other double negative questions that are prominent in other measures such as the Grit-S. As for the ASA, many subjects had difficulty generating stories and whether or not that was related to their attachment patterns or to their ability to tell stories is unclear. This could have influenced the results that were obtained.

CONCLUSION

We are hopeful that a more in depth understanding of the underlying psychological processes of grit can make a contribution to the development of more interventions to improve successful outcomes in a disadvantaged population. The results of this investigation confirm a link between grit and attachment in a disadvantaged high school senior population, where those who are insecurely attached are likely to be less gritty which suggests that an individual's attachment style may be one possible mechanism that can affect an individual's level of grittiness. As studies show that attachment patterns can change and that nurturing attachment relationships can be cultivated (Bakermans-Kranenburg, Van IJzendoorn, & Juffer, 2003; Bernard, Dozier, Bick, & Gordon, 2014; Lieberman & Van Horn, 2009), there is the possibility that influencing attachment patterns may effect change in levels of grit. This study provides a springboard for future research to explore the benefit of relational interventions for adolescents from disadvantaged backgrounds when pursuing long-term goals.

Author Note: I have no financial interest or benefit that will arise from the direct application of this research.

REFERENCES

Ainsworth, M. D. S., Blehar, M. C., Waters, E., & Wall, S. (1978). *Patterns of attachment: A psychological study of the strange situation*. Hillsdale, NJ: Erlbaum.

Ainsworth, M. D.S., & Bowlby, J. (1991). An ethological approach to personality development. *American Psychologist, 46(*4), 333–341.

Allen, J. P. (2008). The attachment system in adolescence. In J. Cassidy & P. R. Shaver (Eds.), *Handbook of attachment: Theory, research, and clinical applications* (2nd ed., pp. 419–435). New York, NY: The Guilford Press.

Allen, J. P., & Miga, E. M. (2010). Attachment in adolescence: A move to the level of emotion regulation. *Journal of Social and Personal Relationships, 27*(2), 181–190. http://dx.doi.org/10.1177/0265407509360898

Alliance For Excellent Education. (2010). High school dropouts in America. Retrieved from www.all4ed.org/files/GraduationRates_FactSheet.pdf

Bakermans-Kranenburg, M. J., Van IJzendoorn, M. H., & Juffer, F. (2003). Less is more: Meta-analyses of sensitivity and attachment interventions in early childhood. *Psychological Bulletin, 129*(2), 195–215. http://dx.doi.org/10.1037/0033-2909.129.2.195

Bartholomew, K., & Horowitz, L. M. (1991). Attachment styles among young adults: A test of a four-category model. *Journal of Personality and Social Psychology, 61*(2), 226–244.

Bernard, K., Dozier, M., Bick, J., & Gordon, M. K. (2015). Intervening to enhance cortisol regulation among children at risk for neglect: Results of a randomized clinical trial. *Development and Psychopathology, 27,* 829–841. doi:10.1017/S095457941400073X

Blair, C., Granger, D. A., Willoughby, M., Mills-Koonce, R., Cox, M., Greenberg, M. T., et al. (2011). Salivary cortisol mediates effects of poverty and parenting on executive functions in early childhood. *Child Development, 82,* 1970–1984. http://dx.doi.org/10.1111/j.1467-8624.2011.01643.x

Bowlby, J. (1973). *Attachment and loss: Vol. II. Separation and anger*. New York, NY: Basic Books.

Brennan, K. A., Clark, C. L., & Shaver, P. R. (1998). Self-report measurement of adult attachment: An integrative overview. In J. A. Simpson & W. S. Rholes (Eds.), *Attachment theory and close relationships* (pp. 46–76). New York, NY: The Guilford Press.

Bretherton, I. (1987). New perspectives on attachment relations: Security, communication, and working models. In J. Osofsky (Ed.), *Handbook of infant development* (2nd ed., pp. 1061–1100). New York, NY: Wiley.

Cassidy, J. (1994). Emotion regulation: Influences of attachment relationships. *Monographs of the*

Society for Research in Child Development, 59(2/3), 228–249. http://dx.doi.org/10.1111/j.1540-5834.1994.tb01287.x

Coppola, G., Vaughn, B. E., Cassibba, R., & Constantini, A. (2006). The attachment script representation procedure in an Italian sample: Associations with adult attachment interview scales and with maternal sensitivity. *Attachment & Human Development, 8*(3), 209–219. http://dx.doi.org/10.1080/14616730600856065

Diamond, L. M., & Fagundes, C. P. (2008). Developmental perspectives on links between attachment and affect regulation over the lifespan. In R. V. Kail (Ed.), *Advances in child development and behavior* (Vol. 36, pp. 83–134). San Diego, CA: Elsevier.

Duckworth, A. L., Peterson, C., Matthews, M. D., & Kelly, D. R. (2007). Grit: Perseverance and passion for long-term goals. *Journal of Personality and Social Psychology, 92,* 1087–1101. http://dx.doi.org/10.1037/0022-3514.92.6.1087

Duckworth, A. L., & Quinn, P. (2009). Development and validation of the short grit scale (GRIT-S). *Journal of Personality Assessment, 91*(2), 166–174. http://dx.doi.org/10.1080/00223890802634290

Duckworth, A. L., & Carlson, S. M. (2013). Self-regulation and school success. In B. W. Sokol, F. M. E. Grouzet, & U. Müller (Eds.), *Self-regulation and autonomy: Social and developmental dimensions of human conduct* (pp. 208–230). New York, NY: Cambridge University Press.

Duckworth, A. L., Kim, B., Tsukayama, E. (2013). Life stress impairs self-control in early adolescence. *Frontiers in Psychology*, 3, article 608, 1–12. http://dx.doi.org/10.3389/fpsyg.2012.00608

Duckworth, A., & Gross, J. J. (2014). Self-control and grit: Related but separable determinants of success. *Current Directions in Psychological Science,* 1–7. http://dx.doi.org/10.1177/0963721414541462

Duckworth, A. (2016). *Grit: The power of passion and perseverance.* New York, NY: Scribner.

Duckworth, A. L., & Seligman, M. E. P. (2017). The science and practice of self-control. *Perspectives on Psychological Science, 12*(5), 715–718. https://doi.org/10.1177/1745691617690880

Dykas, M. J., Woodhouse, S. S., Cassidy, J., & Waters, H. S. (2006). Narrative assessment of attachment representations: Links between secure base scripts and adolescent attachment.

Attachment and Human Development, 8(3), 221–240. http://dx.doi.org/10.1080/14616730600856099

Eisenberg, N., Duckworth, A. L., Spinrad, T. L., & Valiente, C. (2014). Conscientiousness: Origins in childhood. *Developmental Psychology, 50*(5), 1331–1349. http://dx.doi.org/10.1037/a0030977

Enlow, M. B., Egeland, B., Carlson, E., Blood, E., & Wright, R. J. (2014). Mother-infant attachment and the intergenerational transmission of posttraumatic stress disorder. *Development and Psychopathology, 26*(1), 41–65. http://dx.doi.org/10.1017/s0954579413000515

Eskreis-Winkler, L., Shulman, E. P., Beal, S. A., & Duckworth, A. L. (2014). The grit effect: predicting retention in the military, the workplace, school and marriage. *Frontiers in Psychology, 5*(36), 1–12. doi:10.3389/fpsyg.2014.00036

Evans, G. W. (2003). A multimethodological analysis of cumulative risk and allostatic load among rural children. *Developmental Psychology, 39*(5), 924–933. http://dx.doi.org/10.1037/0012-1649.39.5.924

Evans, G. W., Kim, P., Ting, A. H., Tesher, H. B., & Shannis, D. (2007). Cumulative risk, maternal responsiveness, and allostatic load among young adolescents. *Developmental Psychology, 43*(2), 341–351. http://dx.doi.org/10.1037/0012-1649.43.2.341

Evans, G. W., Schamberg, M. A., & McEwen, B. S. (2009). Childhood poverty, chronic stress, and adult working memory. *Proceedings of the National Academy of Sciences of the United States of America, 106*(16), 6545–6549. http://dx.doi.org/10.1073/pnas.0811910106

Gilliom, M., Shaw, D. S., Beck, J. E., Schonberg, M. A., & Lukon, J. L. (2002). Anger regulation in disadvantaged preschool boys: Strategies, antecedents, and the development of self-control. *Developmental Psychology, 38*(2), 222–235. http://dx.doi.org/10.1037/0012-1649.38.2.222

Gunnar, M. R., Brodersen, L., Nachmias, M., Buss, K., & Rigatuso, J. (1996). Stress reactivity and attachment security. *Developmental Psychobiology, 29*(3), 191–204. http://dx.doi.org/10.1002/(sici)1098-2302(199604)29:3%3C191::aid-dev1%3E3.3.co;2-t

Gunnar, M., & Quevedo, K. (2007). The neurobiology of stress and development. *Annual Review of Clinical Psychology, 58,* 145–173. http://dx.doi.org/10.1146/annurev.psych.58.110405.085605

Hazan, C., & Shaver, P. (1987). Romantic love conceptualized as an attachment process. *Journal of Personality and Social Psychology, 52,* 511–524

Heckman, J. J., & Rubinstein, Y. (2001). The importance of noncognitive skills: Lessons from the GED testing program. *American Economic Review, 91*(2), 145–149. http://dx.doi.org/10.1257/aer.91.2.145

Heckman, J. J. (2006). Skill formation and the economics of investing in disadvantaged children. *Science, 312*(5782), 1900–1902. http://dx.doi.org/10.1126/science.1128898

Jensen, F. E., & Nutt, A. E. (2015). *The teenage brain: A neuroscientist's survival guide to raising adolescents and young adults.* New York, NY: HarperCollins.

Kobak, R. (1999). The emotional dynamics of disruptions in attachment relationships: Implications for theory, research, and clinical intervention. In J. Cassidy, & P. R. Shaver (Eds.), *Handbook of attachment: Theory, research, and clinical applications* (pp. 21–43). New York, NY: Guilford Press.

Kobak, R., Cassidy, J., Lyons-Ruth, K., & Ziv, Y. (2006). Attachment, stress, and psychopathology: A developmental pathways model. In D. Cicchetti & D. J. Cohen (Eds.), *Developmental psychopathology: Vol. 1. Theory and method* (pp. 333–369). Hoboken, NJ: Wiley.

Kopp, C. B. (1982). Antecedents of self-regulation: A developmental perspective. *Developmental Psychology, 18*(2), 199–214. https://doi.org/10.1037/0012-1649.18.2.199

Leonhardt, D. (2013, March 16). Better colleges failing to lure talented poor. *The New York Times.* Retrieved from www.nytimes.com.

Levy, J. M., & Steele, H. (2011). Attachment and grit: Exploring possible contributions of attachment styles (from past and present life) to the adult personality construct of grit. *Journal of Social and Psychological Sciences, 4*(2), 16–49.

Lieberman, A. F., & Van Horn, P. (2009). Giving voice to the unsayable: Repairing the effects of trauma in infancy and early childhood. *Child and Adolescent Psychiatric Clinics of North America, 18*(3), 707–720. http://dx.doi.org/10.1016/j.chc.2009.02.007

MacCann, C., & Roberts, R. D. (2010). Do time management, grit, and self-control relate to academic achievement independently of conscientiousness? In R. Hicks (Ed.), *Personality and individual differences: Current directions* (pp. 79–90). Australia: Australian Academic Press.

Main, M., Kaplan, N., & Cassidy, J. (1985). Security in infancy, childhood, and adulthood: A move to the level of representation. *Monographs of the Society for Research in Child Development, 50*(1/2), 66–104. http://dx.doi.org/10.2307/3333827

Main, M., & Solomon, J. (1990). Procedures for identifying infants as disorganized/disoriented during the Ainsworth Strange Situation. In M. T. Greenberg, D. Ciccetti, & E. M. Cummings (Eds.), *Attachment in the preschool years: theory, research, and intervention* (pp. 121–160). Chicago, IL: The University of Chicago Press.

Main, M. (1995). Recent studies in attachment: overview, with selected implications for clinical work. In S. Goldberg, R. Muir, R., & J. Kerr (Eds.), *Attachment theory: Social, developmental, and clinical perspectives* (pp. 407–474). Hillsdale, NJ: Erlbaum.

Main, M., Hesse, E., & Kaplan, N. (2005). Predictability of attachment behavior and representational processes at 1, 6, and 19 years of age: The Berkeley Longitudinal Study. In K. E. Grossman, K. Grossman, & E. Waters (Eds.), *Attachment from infancy to adulthood: The major longitudinal studies* (pp. 245–304). New York, NY: The Guilford Press.

McLoyd, V. C. (1990). The impact of economic hardship on Black families and children: Psychological distress, parenting, and socioemotional development. *Child Development, 61*(2), 311–346. http://dx.doi.org/10.2307/1131096

Mikulincer, M., & Florian, V. (1998). The relationship between adult attachment styles and emotional and cognitive reactions to stressful events. In J. A. Simpson & W. S. Rholes (Eds.), *Attachment theory and close relationships* (pp. 143–165). New York, NY: The Guilford Press.

Mikulincer, M., Shaver, P. R., & Berant, E. (2013). An attachment perspective on therapeutic processes and outcomes. *Journal of Personality,* 1–11. http://dx.doi.org/10.1111/j.1467-6494.2012.00806.x

Putnam, R. D. (2015). *Our kids: The American dream in crisis.* New York, NY: Simon & Schuster.

Reeves, R. V., Venator, J., & Howard, K. (2014, October 22). The character factor: Measures and impact of drive and prudence. Retrieved from http://www.brookings.edu/~/media/research/files/papers/2014/10/22-character-factor-opportunity-reeves/the-character-factor.pdf

Richter, L. M. (2006). Studying adolescence. *Science, 312*(5782), 1902–1905. doi:10.1126/science.1127489

Rindfuss, R. R. (1991). The young adult years: Diversity, structural change, and fertility. *Demography, 28*(4), 493–512. https://doi.org/10.2307/2061419

Robertson-Kraft, C., & Duckworth, A. L. (2014) True grit: Trait-level perseverance and passion for long-term goals predicts effectiveness and retention among novice teachers. *Teachers College Record,* 116 (3), 1–27.

Roisman, G. I., Holland, A., Fortuna, K., Fraley, R. C., Clausell, E., & Clarke, A. (2007). The adult attachment interview and self-reports of attachment style: An empirical rapprochement. *Journal of Personality and Social Psychology, 92*(4), 678–697. http://dx.doi.org/10.1037/0022-3514.92.4.678

Rojas, J. P., Reser, J. A., Usher, E. L., & Toland, M. D. (2012). *Psychometric properties of the academic grit scale.* Lexington, KY: University of Kentucky.

Sapolsky, R. M. (2004). *Why zebras don't get ulcers: The acclaimed guide to stress, stress-related diseases, and coping* (3rd ed.). New York, NY: St. Martin's Griffin.

Shaver, P. R., & Mikulincer, M. (2002). Attachment-related psychodynamics. *Attachment & Human Development, 4*(2), 133–161. http://dx.doi.org/10.1080/14616730210154171

Shaver, P. R., & Mikulincer, M. (2006). Adult attachment strategies and the regulation of emotion. In J. J. Gross (Ed.) *Handbook of emotion regulation* (pp. 446–465). New York, NY: Guilford Press.

Shaver, P. R., & Mikulincer, M. (2008). Adult attachment and affect regulation. In J. Cassidy & P. R. Shaver (Eds.), *Handbook of attachment: Theory, research, and clinical applications* (pp. 503–531). New York, NY: Guilford Press.

Shaver, P. R., & Mikulincer, M. (2009). An overview of adult attachment theory. In J. H. Obegi & E. Berant (Eds.), *Attachment theory and research in clinical work with adults* (pp. 17–45), New York, NY: Guilford Press.

Silk, J. S., Shaw, D. S., Skuban, E. M., Oland, A.A., & Kovacs, M. (2006). Emotion regulation strategies in offspring of childhood-onset depressed mothers. *Journal of Child Psychology and Psychiatry, 47*(1), 69–78. http://dx.doi.org/10.1111/j.1469-7610.2005.01440.x

Spangler, G., & Grossman, K. E. (1993). Biobehavioral organization in securely and insecurely attached infants. *Child Development, 64*(5), 1439–1450. http://dx.doi.org/10.1111/j.1467-8624.1993.tb02962.x

Spear, L. P. (2000). The adolescent brain and age-related behavioral manifestations. *Neuroscience and Biobehavioral Reviews, 24*(4), 417–463. http://dx.doi.org/10.1016/s0149-7634(00)00014-2

Sroufe, L. A., Egeland, B., Carlson, E. A., & Collins, W. A. (2005). *The development of the person: The Minnesota study of risk and adaptation from birth to adulthood.* New York, NY: The Guilford Press.

Steele, R. D., Waters, T. E. A., Bost, K. K., Vaughn, B. E., Truitt, W., Waters, H. S., Booth-LaForce, C., & Roisman, G. I. (2014). Caregiving antecedents of secure base script knowledge: A comparative analysis of young adult attachment representations. *Developmental Psychology, 50*(11), 2526–2538. http://dx.doi.org/10.1037/a0037992

Steinberg, L. (2014). *Age of opportunity: Lessons from the new science of adolescence.* New York, NY: Mariner Books.

Stillwell, R., & Sable, J. (2013). Public School Graduates and Dropouts from the Common Core of Data: School Year 2009–10: First Look (Provisional Data) (NCES 2013–309). Washington, DC: U.S. Department of Education, National Center for Education Statistics. Retrieved March 14, 2013, from http://nces.ed.gov/pubsearch

Tagney, J. P., Baumeister, R. F., & Boone, A. L. (2004). High self-control predicts good adjustment, less pathology, better grades, and interpersonal success. *Journal of Personality, 72*(2), 271–322. doi:10.1111/j.0022-3506.2004.00263.x

Tough, P. (2012). *How children succeed: Grit, curiosity, and the hidden power of character.* New York, NY: Houghton Mifflin Harcourt.

Tough, P. (2016, May 21). To help kids thrive, coach their parents. *The New York Times.* Retrieved from http://www.nytimes.com

Wadsworth, M. E., & Berger, L. E. (2006). Adolescents coping with poverty-related family stress: Predictors of coping and psychological symptoms. *Journal of Youth and Adolescence, 35*(1), 57–70. http://dx.doi.org/10.1007/s10964-005-9022-5

Walker, E. F., Walder, D. J., & Reynolds, R. (2001). Developmental changes in cortisol secretion in normal and at-risk youth. *Development and Psychopathology*, *13*, 721–732. http://dx.doi.org/10.1017/s0954579401003169

Waters, H. S., & Rodrigues-Doolabh, L. (2001, April). Are attachment scripts the building blocks of attachment representations? Narrative assessment of representations and the AAI. In H. Waters & E. Waters (Chairs), Narrative measures of attachment for adults. *Poster symposium presented at the Biennial Meetings of the Society for Research in Child Development*, Minneapolis, MN.

Waters, H. S., & Waters, E. (2006). The attachment working models concept: Among other things, we build script-like representations of secure base experiences. *Attachment and Human Development*, 8(3), 185–197. http://dx.doi.org/10.1080/14616730600856016

Wei, M., Russell, D. W., Mallinckrodt, B., & Zakalik, R. A. (2004). Cultural equivalence of adult attachment across four ethnic groups: Factor structure, structured means, and associations with negative mood. *Journal of Counseling Psychology*, *51*(4), 408–417. http://dx.doi.org/10.1037/0022-0167.51.4.408

Wei, M., Russell, D. W., Mallinckrodt, B., & Vogel, D. L. (2007). The Experiences in Close Relationship Scale (ECR)-Short form: Reliability, validity and factor structure. *Journal of Personality Assessment*, *88*(2), 187–204. http://dx.doi.org/10.1080/00223890701268041

Wolters, C. A., & Hussain, M. (2015). Investigating grit and its relations with college students' self-regulated learning and academic achievement. *Metacognition and Learning*, *10*(3), 293–311. https://doi.org/10.1007/s11409-014-9128-9

How to Raise Kind Kids: And Get Respect, Gratitude, and a Happier Family in the Bargain (2018), by Thomas Lickona. New York: Penguin Books.

David Streight
heartofcharacter.org

In the introduction to this, his latest book, Tom Lickona tells a story about the man who taught a parenting class. He called his class Ten Commandments for Parents. People came from far and wide to benefit from what he shared. The man got married, and soon he and his wife experienced the joy of seeing their first-born enter the world. A couple of years with this child led to the teacher's felt need to downsize his syllabus. He called the updated version Five Suggestions for Parents. At about this time, child number two blessed their lives, and as that second child entered toddlerhood—the older sibling now in early childhood—the teacher thought deeply about his course and ceded to the need for further changes. He now focused on Three Tentative Hints for Parents. When a third child came along, the man stopped teaching altogether.

It's not just a nice story with a tad too much truth for those of us with more than one child—or for any parent or educator who's been around long enough to observe families—it's a fitting beginning for a book with the lofty aspirations of that teacher's initial course, yet written by a man with the humility that develops somewhere between child two and child three. To our good fortune, Tom Lickona is a father of two; he never stopped teaching.

Tom Lickona needs no introduction for the vast majority of the *Journal of Character Education* readers. For newer readers, he was for more than 40 years a professor of education at the State University of New York at Cortland, a key figure in the foundation and ongoing work of the Character Education Partnership (now Character.org), and founder of the Center for the Fourth and Fifth Rs (Respect and Responsibility), which he continues to direct. More germane to this Journal, Tom Lickona is perhaps the best known character educator in the Western world (some might say the rest of the world, too). *How to Raise Kind Kids* is his ninth authored or coauthored title—and in the eyes of this writer, his best thus far. It is his second book for parents, following the 1983 publication of *Raising Good Children: Helping Your Child through the Stages of Moral Development—From Birth Through the Teenage Years*.

Journal of Character Education, Volume 14(1), 2018, pp. 75–77
Copyright © 2018 Information Age Publishing, Inc.
ISSN 1543-1223

There is a second reason why that teacher's story so fittingly introduces this gem of a book. It is a metaphor—albeit incomplete—for the threads that run through the book so tightly. *How to Raise Kind Kids* benefits certainly from experience accumulated by a writer not only with children of his own, but with a host of grandchildren he has clearly spent ample time with. Beyond experience, the book is a product of wisdom, the wisdom gleaned in professional practice as a psychologist/educator, and that handed down by the sages of old and more recent times: the classic Greek philosophers on molding character, Cicero on gratitude and self-control, and later voices like the altruism of Samuel and Pearl Oliner and the insights of Mark Twain. But intertwined with personal experience and wisdom, the thread of scholarship runs equally as strong: Lickona supports his recommendations with the data from large surveys, the research findings of tightly constructed experiments, and recent neurological studies.

Per the author's suggestion, *How to Raise Kind Kids* can be read "in whatever way you feel is most useful." Though there is a logical progression, Lickona points out that he wrote his chapters to stand alone—the reader can feel free to jump to whatever seems most interesting (or perhaps most pressing). Several chapters in the latter half of the book focus on issues of a specific nature that might draw parents because of something happening in a child's life or in the wider society. "Getting Control of Screens" (Chapter 9) or "Helping Your Kids Avoid the Dangers of a Hypersexualized Culture—and Find True Love" (Chapter 15) are examples of topics parents in the Internet age might feel an immediate need to jump to. These chapters and those that surround them—on the value of family meetings, on how to have difficult conversations, on how to diminish complaining while increasing gratitude—are to my mind the strongest in the book because of their myriad wonderful suggestions. After a first reading, I tried to review mentally, in attempting an educated guess about how many truly feasible, practical suggestions Lickona offers: is it hundreds, or only scores? I planned to keep track in a second reading (well over a hundred is a truer estimate than scores), but I soon lost track, falling victim to the book's many engaging anecdotes and examples.

Lickona's invitation to read-as-deemed-useful notwithstanding—and despite the fact that practical suggestions await in these latter chapters—I am in favor of a more traditional procedure, starting from the beginning. I say this because the early chapters of *How to Raise Kind Kids* touch at the real heart of the matter. Readers who jump ahead in search of specific suggestions or possible solutions risk missing out on what Tom Lickona does best here, that is, ground specific parental concerns in a purpose-focused rationale. He wants his readers to immerse themselves in all-important questions like "What can we do to nudge our children out of their comfort zone when being kind takes courage?" and—probably first and foremost—"the most important question we can ask ourselves … What kind of person do we want our child to be?"

Our job as parents is, after all, to "feed our children's capacity for kindness"; kindness is the ultimate goal. Specific strategies to liberate children from video distractions or to diminish complaints certainly make life better for family members, but these specific improvements, albeit welcome, are only incidentals in the quest for what Lickona sees as essential for what we and our society need: a family culture where all members are challenged to live up to a high ideal. The greatest loss in jumping to chapters of immediate concern without taking a more holistic look at this essence is that of missing out on things like "your single most important tool for building a positive family culture," a phrase Lickona uses to refer to family meetings, on why they are so important and on the effects such meetings can have on families. This chapter sits both in the conceptual heart of the book and, precisely, at its geographic heart, as the eighth of 15 chapters. It would be a shame to risk missing it.

Given that Chapter 8 includes "tips" for the success of meetings, I could not help wonder if the Lickona family's earliest forays into the practice did not follow a restricted number of "tentative hints" some predecessor had passed along, and then—in the light of their experience—if perhaps those hints grew to perhaps five more solid "suggestions" worthy of transmission. In contrast to the fate of the Ten Commandments the parenting teacher started his career with, Lickona's more humbly outlined "Ten Tips for a Good Family Meeting" represent a magnificent—and probably enduring—blend of best practices in a variety of fields, from group process to collaborative problem solving to 21st century classroom management and the latest recommendations for facilitating moral development.

In an early chapter, Lickona sets the tone with the story a grandfather tells. It is the epic battle between two wolves: the wolf of cruelty and anger and the wolf of kindness and peace. To his grandson's question about who will win, the grandfather replies "the one you feed." Suffice it to say that *How to Raise Kind Kids: And Get Respect, Gratitude, and a Happier Family in the Bargain* is nourishment for the wolf we want to win. None of Tom Lickona's family meeting tips—or any of the several other thoughtful suggestions that so enrich this book—is a hard, fast, guaranteed prescription for instant success. But unlike the parenting class instructor, most of us, parents or educators, do not have the luxury of quitting when the going gets tough or doubts set in. *How to Raise Kind Kids* has much to replenish ideas and keep hopes high.

David Streight is a school psychologist currently serving as Resident Scholar at heartofcharacter.org

CPSIA information can be obtained
at www.ICGtesting.com
Printed in the USA
FSHW02n1825031018
52696FS